MORE POEMS ABOUT RUCKSACKS AND PHONES

MORE POEMS ABOUT RUCKSACKS AND PHONES

STEVE MINGLE

MORE POEMS ABOUT RUCKSACKS AND PHONES

©2024, Steve Mingle

The right of Steve Mingle to be identified as the author of this work has been asserted in accordance with the Copyright, Design and Patents Act 1988.

All Rights Reserved. No part of this book may be reproduced in any form, by photocopying or by any electronic or mechanical means, including information storage or retrieval systems, without permission from the Copyright owner.

ISBN 978-1-916838-54-3

First published 2024
Printed and bound in Great Britain by Biddles Books Ltd, King's Lynn

Contents

What The Fuck Is Going On?   6

You've Got To Start Somewhere   8
Fifteen Minutes Of Fame; No Chips; Pictures Of Your Dinner

Rants   17
White Van Man; Deliveroo Bastard; Personal Trainer; Doctor's Receptionist; Smartphone Wanker; Smartphone Wanker (alternative verses); That Smug Twat Who Reads The News on ITV; Old Man With Anger Management Issues Vs Automated Checkout Machine In Marks and Spencers; Don't Buy A Dyson; Rucksack Cunt: Premature Christmas Twat

Nostalgia   43
Ashton Market (Part One); Maine Road Matchday '69: Reasons To Be Nostalgic, Part 1; Ashton Market (Part Two)

Heroes And Villains   59
Frank; Spanish Dave; Five Years; The Ballad Of Desperate Don; He's Boris; Neville

Lockdown   72
Wear A Mask You Selfish...Person; Relentless; Amazing; Worse Things Happen At Sea

That's Just Silly   85
King Dong; Pure Cremation TV; Imadickhead.com; Celebrity Shags; Man Flu; I'm An Accountant; Jurgen Klopp's Teeth; Me House Is On Fire; Televisual Feast; The Bride Of Dracula

Acknowledgements and other stuff   110

WHAT THE FUCK IS GOING ON...?

In the event that any of my old English teachers are still alive and remember me – both of which are pretty bloody unlikely – they might be surprised to find that I've put together an anthology of what might loosely be described as poetry. It wasn't that I was terrible at English, more that, as one of my school reports said, I showed "a very discriminating interest" in what they were trying to teach me. And I absolutely hated poetry. The stuff we were bullied into reading in class left me totally cold. All of it.

The only poetry to make any kind of positive impact appeared in Monty Python's Big Red Book (the one with the blue cover, obviously). Neatly positioned between The Ministry Of Silly Walks and the epic saga of Doug and Dinsdale Piranha - the gangland supremos who terrorised the East End with their deadly combination of brutality and sarcasm - were "The poems of Ewen McTeagle". Classics such as "Lend us a quid till the end of the week" and "Can I have £50 to mend the shed" were gloriously banal but what I really loved was the accompanying critical fawning, ascribing some intellectual merit to these pathetic efforts. It was the Pythons' parody of the pretentiousness surrounding poetry that really appealed, because that was just how I felt about so much of what had been force-fed to me in class. Why are you trying to read all these sophisticated nuances into this simplistic drivel? I just didn't get it.

Then, a few years later, within the punk rock movement, came a man who demonstrated that there was a form of poetry that might appeal even to complete philistines like me. John Cooper Clarke's emergence was a revelation. He was clever, charismatic and funny, and blessed with that wonderfully distinctive voice. What struck me most about his work was how his brilliant rhyming gave it both rhythm and humour and allowed him to deliver his words at a startling pace, further enhancing their impact. This was poetry for the common man, and I loved it.

Fast forward just the forty years. I was happily retired from work and didn't miss office life one bit. But what I did miss was the adrenalin rush of standing on a platform talking at people, which I'd manipulated into becoming a big part of my job. I wanted to rediscover that buzz. But how?

I can't sing. I can't play any musical instrument. I'm hopeless at telling jokes. My options were limited. But after seeing JCC yet again – by this time as much a stand-up comic as a poet, and a bloody funny one – I decided, purely for personal amusement, to have a go at putting together a few pieces of my own. And after years of prevarication, I finally convinced myself that one or two of them weren't that bad, and that maybe I should have a go at inflicting them on strangers.

The handful of poems I started out with were intended to be funny, so I had to decide whether to go for a comedy night or a spoken word event. I went down the comedy route. What's the worst that can happen? That people don't laugh at all and you get no reaction. And that's exactly what did happen. But it happened to every other act as well. It was a night where people went to a comedy evening determined not to laugh at anything, as if conceding that something was funny was a sign of weakness. "Come on then, make me laugh!" I was a bit surprised; after all, this was Manchester, not Yorkshire.

I wasn't too downhearted – no-one had thrown anything at me or yelled. "Get off!" and I still had the backstop of spoken word nights to try. But I was at the bar towards the end of the night and asked the barman "Is it always like this?" He said it was just one of those nights, but if it was any consolation he thought that I was the funniest act of the evening. This wasn't exactly saying a lot but the fact that he thought I wasn't terrible was a proper boost. It was enough to convince me that there might just be an audience for my kind of stuff, even if it could be accommodated on a park bench. And sometimes a little bit of encouragement is all it takes.

So started an adventure of spouting profanities at spoken word, comedy and open mic nights, at venues all around Greater Manchester - and a few beyond - discovering a new world populated by sometimes weird but often wonderfully talented people and finding a new passion in my retirement years. And every now and then I get asked whether I've got an anthology available. So for those people kind enough to have enquired – what follows is all your fault.

YOU'VE GOT TO START SOMEWHERE

The material I'd managed to put together prior to braving the general public was a right old ragbag. It incorporated plenty of half-baked ideas, some of which still haven't been converted into completed poems and probably never will be. And a few more that did get finished but which no-one seemed to like. Least of all me. But there were a few that have somehow stood the test of time and which I still perform every now and then even though they feel like relics from a bygone age.

Fifteen Minutes Of Fame

This is the first piece I ever performed. It's about the truly abominable Jeremy Kyle Show and the people who chose to appear on it. I never actually watched a full episode (honest) but trailers and snippets were more than enough to generate sorrowful shakes of the head and mutterings along the lines of, "What is the world coming to...?"

A few months later, the show was taken off air and I thought that would see the poem cast into the archives of oblivion, as I assumed no-one would relate to it anymore. I tried to extend its relevant life by tacking an extra verse on at the end but I needn't have bothered, as it quickly became apparent that people would always remember this show, being as it was a low-water mark in British popular culture.

9.30 in the morning, every day
The dregs of society are on display
On a TV programme that's truly vile
With its knowing host, Mr Kyle
Losers, bruisers, strip-joint cruisers
Dysfunctional dropouts from back-street boozers
Desperately seeking humiliation
In front of a voyeuristic nation
No hope or ambition, their only aim
Is to grab their fifteen minutes of fame

Got a text from the missus saying she'd be home late
She was off out clubbing with her hideous mate
So I went round her house and shagged her mother
Who came highly recommended by my little brother
Now her mum's up the duff and she says it's mine
But if I move in with her it'd all be fine
Couldn't decide who to go with, so we went on TV
Where the audience insisted it's the mother for me
So if it all goes tits up, at least I'm not to blame
And we lapped up our fifteen minutes of fame

I suspected my wife was having a fling
With a supercool rasta dripping with bling
And I knew for sure I was on the right track
When our newborn baby came out black
She said, "There's no need for consternation
It must be an accident of pigmentation"
So we sat on the sofa in studio five
While the DNA test results were read out - live
Now that bitch and her sprog won't be bearing my name
But at least I've had fifteen minutes of fame

My girlfriend doesn't wanna see me no more
Since she caught me having sex with our labrador
People might think what I did was wrong
But you should see what it can do with its tongue
I didn't set out with any dubious intention
It was just another case of canine intervention
She was gonna sell the story to the Daily Mail
Unless I told the viewers the sorry tale
Of how the family pet ended up lame
So the dog got its fifteen minutes of fame

I don't normally gamble but I wouldn't mind betting
That every single participant's a certified cretin
With a studio audience specially selected
For having brains that even the police force rejected
It's frightening that this show even exists
Let alone topping daytime viewing lists
Have we got nothing better to do with our days
Than watch car crash TV in a hungover haze
It's the great British public that's really to blame
For giving these morons fifteen minutes of fame

Tragedy ended the show, sorry to say
"And not before time", cried folk who'd watched every day
It was taken off air, quite rightly of course
But the me-too brigade were soon out in force
"I never thought he'd try to make me look like a dick
I came out of the studio feeling physically sick"
"I never imagined it'd be like this
Ever since I was on it people just take the piss"
Come on boys, give it a fucking rest
You're just after a few bob from the gutter press
There was so much spouting of bollocks and bile
I almost felt sorry for Jeremy Kyle
Almost but not quite
'Cos he should forever hang his head in shame
For exploiting our craving for fifteen minutes of fame

No Chips

The cycle of sustained overindulgence, then dieting first with "this time it'll be different" zeal but then with gradually diminishing commitment, before finally giving up and slowly reverting to another phase of excessive consumption is an all-too familiar one for lots of us. I do know a few people who manage to be sensible all year round, but where's the fun in that?

No chips – I'm on a diet
It really works, you ought to try it
I've now survived for fifteen days
Without a trace of mayonnaise
I used to get my five a day
From a bottle of Chardonnay
Now it's organic runner beans
Broccoli and clementines
Once I thought that nothing beats a
Deep-pan pepperoni pizza
But now for dinner I love to eat a…
…Chicken salad with two Ryvita?

No chips – I'm on a diet
Grill it, steam it, just don't fry it
Eating stuff that's cooked in lard
Will only make your arteries hard
Resist that cod in greasy batter
It's simply mind over matter
Don't tuck into that pork pie, you prat
It's full of saturated fat
Just a chunk of Stilton or Red Leicester'll
Raise your level of bad cholesterol
And if that kebab slides down your throat
You'll end up like Mr Creosote

No chips – I'm on a diet
Haven't you cynics all gone quiet?
It's worth coping with a little hunger
To make yourself look ten years' younger
I've got my GP off my back
And slashed my risk of heart attack
By carefully watching what I eat
Now I can almost see my feet

No chips – I'm on a diet
It's getting tough, I can't deny it
It's hard to keep that willpower strong
When you're bloody ravenous all day long
Six weeks of eating things I hate
And I've still not reached my target weight
It gets tougher day by day
To resist that Chinese takeaway
And surely it can't really hurt
If I sneak in the odd dessert?
Treacle tart, spotted dick
Lashings of custard, nice and thick
Last night in bed I fantasised...
...About Mr Kipling's apple pies?

More chips - fuck the diet!
Happiness, you just can't buy it
What's the point of being thin
If you're as miserable as sin
My wife's now living up the smoke
She left me for some chubby bloke
My calorie-controlled obsession
Had plunged her into deep depression
So if you're feeling slightly lardy
And you'd rather be more Laurel than Hardy
Although your doc might not endorse it...
...Just squeeze yourself into a corset

Pictures Of Your Dinner

This is not so much a poem as a public health service announcement. It provides essential, potentially life-saving advice about how to eliminate the risk of food poisoning when travelling abroad.

It must have been the 1990s when I first began to equate dodgy foreign food aimed at hapless tourists with the practice of displaying an illustrated laminated menu at the entrance to a restaurant. The menus would invariably be dog-eared and the photographs bleached from exposure to the sun. And the food they depicted inevitably turned out to be scarcely fit for human consumption. This is something that, like so many others, I had to learn the hard way.

Ignore this advice at your peril...

It's hard to know which one to choose
The restaurant with the best reviews
Or the one which sells the cheapest booze?
But the places that you must avoid
Feature output from a polaroid
Cos your digestive system will be destroyed
If you dare to venture into an establishment which displays...
Pictures of your dinner

Ignore the ratings on Trip Adviser
They're all fake, and you'll be none the wiser
Till you regurgitate your appetiser
You might only have a toasted sandwich
But your face will soon contort with anguish
Cos "bleaurghhh" is the universal language
Spoken fluently by everyone who's made the cardinal error of dining where they show...
Pictures of your dinner

A passing tourist said "that looks nice
A lovely chicken curry with rice"
It's already been recycled twice
Then the waiter came across to tell her
To try the strangely luminous paella
Now she's doubled up with salmonella
He said, "The Angus burger's our *tour de force*
It comes with fries and a special sauce"
Turns out Angus was the name of horse
Whose reconstituted and inadequately defrosted flesh made up the botulism bonanza portrayed in misleadingly appetising fashion on the menu which featured...
Pictures of your dinner

Why hasn't the owner been arrested?
They say his kitchen's rat-infested
And the ancient fridge is so congested
That the meat's begun to decompose
But then how else do you suppose
They do three courses for ten euros?
I'd sooner eat my own excrement
Or suffer partial dismemberment
Or spend a week in Stoke-on-Trent
Than eat anywhere that shows...
Pictures of your dinner

By now it should be crystal clear
That vomiting and diarrhoea
Are on the menu if you eat here
Though for bulimics it's the perfect dinner
Cos you're guaranteed to end up thinner
But be aware that what killed Michael Winner
Was misguidedly taking a break from reviewing his usual posh Michelin star gaffs and instead investigating how common people live by dining just once at a restaurant which showed...
Pictures of your dinner

So you might think, "Well, that looks alright"
But you should be running off with fright
'Cos all it takes is just a bite
To have you chucking up all night
And it's no use being all contrite
'Cos it'll serve you bloody right
For being so utterly, mindlessly and unforgiveably stupid as to eat anywhere where they show...
Pictures of your dinner

RANTS

I'm quite an angry person really. I think I've always had it inside me, but it's definitely come out more frequently as the years have rolled by. So much of the modern world has become increasingly difficult for me to make sense of. I think it's just part of the natural cycle of life. And when you're retired you've got so much more time to find things to get angry about.

Some of it is born at frustration of developments in technology that I struggle to cope with, some comes from the idiotic, moronic, reckless behaviour of members of the general public. Were there as many dickheads in circulation back in the day? Maybe there were, but the emergence of social media means that these days they're far more visible than ever before.

White Van Man

Most drivers have moments when we get distracted or make a slight misjudgement. Maybe we go over the speed limit or nip through the lights just as they turn red. And we feel bad when it happens and give ourselves a bit of a talking to and lock back into concentrating properly. Unless we're a White Van Man. Because when you're a White Van Man, every day is Drive Like A Cunt Day.

This twat thinks he's the king of the road
Pays scant regard to the Highway Code
With tyres so worn they're about to explode
White Van Man's on the loose

He'll cut you up big time and never say sorry
As he rushes back home in time for Corrie
With his cargo direct from the back of a lorry
White Van Man's on the loose

He veers across from lane to lane
Speeds up whenever he nears a chicane
He'll make you wish you'd caught the train
White Van Man's on the loose

Drives like he's just had a skinful of beers
Taps out text messages while he steers
Not much going on between his ears
White Van Man's on the loose

Need to overtake him? Better say a prayer
Who knows what's behind him, he doesn't care
His rear-view mirror's positioned there
For the singular purpose of checking his hair
With air-freshener most unpleasantly scented
His van could be stolen, owned or rented
But the bodywork's always scratched and dented
And a bigger fuckwit's never been invented
Than White Van Man on the loose

He's the driving hazard you love to hate
Can never be arsed to indicate
His cognitive function isn't too great
His eyesight's in a right old state
His brakes are past their sell-by date
His mantra – just intimidate
Please God don't let him procreate
White Van Man's on the loose!

Deliveroo Bastard

One of the most noticeable changes to the landscape of central Manchester after we emerged from lockdown was that it became a far more dangerous place. The roads were tricky enough for pedestrians to navigate as it was, but now we had to contend with a veritable army of Kamikaze cyclists careering around our streets and pavements in a bewilderingly random fashion. And presumably racking up points for every pedestrian they hit.

I'm all for encouraging cycling as a means of keeping fit and reducing vehicle emissions, but I draw the line at this lot. Whenever one goes zapping by you, just point at them and shout "Bastard!" You might get a few funny looks but it'll make you feel better.

When the streets were deserted, they had the run of the town
But now they're crowded again they just mow people down
They all claim to provide an invaluable service
But just the sight of their bikes doesn't half make you nervous
This army of reckless irresponsible jerks
Speed through gaps in the traffic just like Eddy Merckx
Now we're all in the grip of a new reign of terror
Where just crossing the road could be a terminal error
Even the great Bradley Wiggins never went any faster
Than the average Mancunian Deliveroo Bastard

If you dare take a trip to the Northern Quarter
You'll set yourself up as a lamb to the slaughter
As he ploughs through the hordes of *al fresco* drinkers
With the peripheral vision of a horse wearing blinkers
With his insulated box full of local cuisine
He's a one-man pedestrian intimidation machine
"What's all the rush mate?" you hear passers-by say
"They'll have to heat it all up in the oven anyway!"
But Indian or Chinese, burgers or pasta
It all travels at speed with Deliveroo Bastard

No need to wear helmets, they're indestructible
And their bicycle repair costs are tax-deductible
With these guys you need eyes in the back of your head
To them, a no-entry sign means "go straight ahead"
They shoot through the lights like they're red-green colour-blind
Can't imagine you'll see them on Mastermind
Berate 'em, abuse 'em, you're wasting your breath
Take one step off the kerb and you're dicing with death
Just a stroll to your local will end in disaster
If you get in the way of Deliveroo Bastard

Now - where's that bastard got to with me pizza?

Personal Trainer

This one was triggered by a South African guy in a gym that I used to go to. Every morning he'd be there, giving it the Lord Of The Manor and eyeing up all the women. And the platitudes and cliches he'd come out with - very loudly - used to drive me up the wall.

I'm not a happy person in the gym. I go there under sufferance because I can't play as much sport as I used to but I still need exercise to function properly. I'm a bit of a no pain, no gain merchant but when I'm hurting my threshold for losing my rag – already extremely low – means that even the slightest irritation will start me off. And this guy was way more than slightly irritating. Whenever I perform this poem I have a picture of him in my head. Twat.

He makes a killing from folk with no self-motivation
Bores the fuck out of all-comers with his banal conversation
Struts all around the gym like he owns the place
Encroaching on everyone's personal space
Why does this twat have to talk so loud
He's training one person, not a fucking crowd
He's a fitness obsessive through and through
His body mass index never exceeds twenty-two
But then again neither does his IQ
'Cos he's a Personal Trainer

If they think his services are worth the expense
His clients must have got more money than sense
In they trot one by one in their designer kit
Deluding themselves that he'll get them fit
They sit on their arses scrolling through Facebook
They'd burn more calories eating a donut
And though the evidence hardly supports the impression
He tells 'em he's seeing some real progression
So the fuckwits sign up for another ten sessions
With Personal Trainer

Every woman he claps eyes on, he thinks he's in with a chance
But they can tell he's a wanker with a single glance
Whenever he looks in the mirror he falls in love
His body a gift from heaven above
He's an athletic Adonis in pristine health
If he was a chocolate he'd eat himself
In his mind he's the region's premier heartthrob
But everybody he meets knows he's an absolute knob
Just fuck off and get a proper job
Personal Trainer

Doctor's Receptionist

I feel a bit mean picking on NHS employees, but the experience of trying to get an appointment at my doctor's surgery is such a profoundly miserable one that it just encourages you to think that the best remedy for whatever ails you is to do nothing at all and hope it gets better. I know they're under pressure, but aren't we all. When you go to the doc's you're usually nervous and worried, and what you don't need is to be treated with withering contempt by the receptionist, as if you've no right to be in there, disturbing her working day.

The line's engaged yet again, I'm sixteen in the queue
Then I get timed out before I get through
So I end up traipsing to the surgery in person
Before my symptoms have a chance to worsen
She taps away at her keyboard as though I don't exist
And even when I start cursing and shaking me fist
She displays not the slightest sense of urgency
Thank God my condition's not an emergency
At last she says, "Can I help you?" I think, "Evidently not
Cos you're about as much use as a chocolate teapot"
But I'm determined to give it my best shot
With the doctor's receptionist

I say, "Me hip's giving me jip and I've got knackered knees
Can I just have ten minutes with the doctor please?"
But I can tell straight away it's a futile attempt
As her wasp-chewing face exudes total contempt
With her hair tucked up severely in a matronly bun
And the interpersonal skills of Attila the Hun
She looks at me like I've committed a crime
"What the hell are you doing here wasting my time?
You've not got palpitations, your face isn't blue
Your breathing's ok and you've got all your limbs too
The doctor's too busy to see the likes of you"
Says the doctor's receptionist

Her personal objective at the start of each day
Is to keep all prospective patients away
She's like a nightclub bouncer in the rough part of town
"You're not coming in, your name's not down"
The chances of getting an appointment are minimal
In a previous life she was a Nazi war criminal
She sneers down her nose, makes me feel three feet tall
"Just grow a pair loser, you're not poorly at all"
So if my ailments result in that fatal death knell
And I'm assigned a new home in heaven…or hell
My tombstone will read "Told you I wasn't well…"
So fuck you, doctor's receptionist!

Smartphone Wanker

Is there anyone left in the country who isn't one of these? What the fuck is wrong with us all? I get angry with myself for over-using my phone – but there are so many folk out there who make me look like a part-timer.

Jesus Christ, I could do with a drink
I'm stuck on this train, I can't hear myself think
Men and women, girls and boys
Competing to see who can make the most noise
Calling the office, chatting to their mates
Broadcasting intimate details of last night's dates
One phones home, "Hello love, it's only me"
Well who the fucking hell else would it be?
I don't get what this terrible racket's about
Isn't the concept of a phone that there's no need to shout?
In a rare moment of quiet I hear a bloke up the front say
"Blimey, is it National Talk Like A Cunt Day?"
I'd sooner be stuck in a lift with a load of bankers
Than sat in this carriage full of Smartphone Wankers

In a tourist restaurant by the picturesque harbour
Sits a floppy-haired geezer who could do with a barber
I don't get the impression that he's desperately poor
But you'd think he'd never seen a plate of food before
He's got a mangy salad with some plastic ham
But it still finds its way onto Instagram
I said, "Please don't do that, you look such a twat
Who the hell d'you think would be interested in that?"
"I'll have you know it's had fifteen likes already"
"What, from people who still go to bed with a teddy?"
He can't walk ten yards in the port without taking a selfie
But the next one proved to be terminally unhealthy
"Well, have you ever seen a luxury boat like that
I'll just step back for a better angle"…Splat!
He smacked his head on the jetty where the yachts drop anchor
Cause of death – being a Smartphone Wanker

Look at me, look at me, I'm at the gig
I bet you've never seen an artist this big
I'm recording it all, I'm dead close to the stage
But this bloke behind me's in some kind of rage
Every couple of minutes he vents his spleen
"I didn't come here to look at your fucking screen
Keep putting that thing in my eyeline
And I'll ram the fucker where the sun don't shine"
He was the most uncouth fellow I've ever heard
But he did turn out to be true to his word
As a consequence of his mindlessly violent action
A pretty nurse had to perform a rather delicate extraction
I asked if there was any way I could thank her
"Ooh yes please...just stop being a Smartphone Wanker"

There's this bloke in the office who's an absolute jerk
He's ruled by his smartphone, does he do any work?
He circulates a new video almost every minute
"Just look at that, it's hilarious innit!"
No it's not, you crushing bore
We've all seen it umpteen times before
And it wasn't even funny the first time
He's driving at speed when his smartphone pings
With another of those truly wretched things
It's a viral video of a dancing cat
How could anyone resist looking at that?
Watching that moggy strut its stuff wasn't his best decision
Cos his car veered off into a head-on collision
He came off second best to a giant petrol tanker
Goodnight, God bless, Smartphone Wanker

Smartphone Wanker - alternative verses

My methodology for writing Smartphone Wanker was to think of words that rhymed with "wanker", then construct a couplet to finish each verse and go back and develop a scene to lead up to it. But I ended up with seven verses, which even by my standards of excessive dronage was a bit much. So I picked the four I liked the best and the other three were stored away with all the unfinished bits and pieces accumulated over the years. The random couplets, the "that's a nice turn of phrase" snippets that didn't seem to fit anywhere, the half-baked ideas that I just couldn't convert into full-blown poems.

Whenever I delved into this ragbag of misfits, searching for inspiration, these poor discarded verses would look up at me pleading, "Please Uncle Steve, we're not that bad, can we come out tonight?" but every time I inflicted Smartphone Wanker on people I stuck with the original four, largely because I couldn't be bothered to try and learn the others. But because I've got space to fill, I thought I'd let the alternative verses have an outing on paper instead. Whether anyone will ever get to hear them is another question entirely.

Look at me, look at me, I'm at the big game
I know you're watching on telly, but it's not the same
I'm so close to the players, I've taken pictures galore
And when they come back over here I'll take a few more
Now I'll just post this comment on the message board
What's that noise, has somebody scored?
I've got the sporting summer's hottest ticket
I'm at Old Trafford for the Ashes cricket
But I'm so wrapped up in my Facebook feed
That so far I've missed every single wicket
Same thing happened last year, when we played Sri Lanka
It's a way of life when you're a Smartphone Wanker

Security's tight for this sold-out gig
I've never been stuck in a queue this big
But entertaining us all outside the arena
Is a Glaswegian busker with an aggressive demeanour
He's got genuine talent, so he can't really blame us
For recording him, in case he ever gets famous
But as he finishes his song to a round of applause
I realise I've left the button on pause
I say, "That last one was brilliant, ten out of ten
I'd love to record it, would you play it again?"
He says, "What the fuck d'you think this is, *Casablanca*?
Stitch that one up, Smartphone Wanker!"

A hi-tech salesman with product to sell
Went in search of international clientele
He strode down the Strasse on a facetime call
Not paying attention to where he was going at all
He smacked into a lamp-post at such a pace
That his nose got splattered all over his face
So he had to turn up at his important engagement
With his front teeth scattered all over the pavement
He tried to sell his wares in the conference hall
But in that state couldn't get any takers at all
Non merci, no thank you, non gracias, nein danke
No-one does business with a Smartphone Wanker

That Smug Twat Who Reads The News On ITV

It was during lockdown that I consciously stopped watching news on TV - and I've never started again. It's so relentlessly depressing. You can get the headlines from a news app or a two-minute radio bulletin and it's easy to find out more about specific stories and events if you want to. Usually I don't. These days more than ever, it feels like ignorance is bliss – and a bloody sight better for your mental health.

And if the news itself isn't grim enough, then the sight and sound of one particular newsreader is enough to tip anyone over the edge. There are some people where you can tell at a glance that they think they're the whole cheese, and this fella's certainly one of them. I first witnessed him reading the news sometime during lockdown and was absolutely appalled by the mocking tone with which he delivered some story about Trump. And by how funny he thought his little quips and gestures were. What a smug bastard. I didn't disagree with his sentiments but this was News as light entertainment and there are plenty of other shows that do that. I still occasionally see snippets of him and he's worse than ever. Christ knows what he'll be like when we get to election time. Just stick to giving us the facts and leave the smartarse comments to people who know what they're doing.

He thinks he's so wonderfully clever, the TV star with the most
Less a humble newsreader, more a chat show host
He always looks so very pleased with himself
Well if I ever meet him, he'd better fear for his health
Cos I'm not a violent man but I don't mind admitting
He's got the sort of face I'd never tire of hitting
He thinks his minuscule talent has brought him nationwide fame
Well sorry mate, hardly anyone knows your name
And big yourself up all you like but you'll still always be
That smug twat who reads the news on ITV

He's Spare Harry's best mate, well that says it all
And for the blockbuster interview he got the big call
He's the ultimate sycophant, that's why they picked him
To help the prince of self-pity look like a mistreated victim
To hear the poor little rich boy's pathetic bleatings
You'd think he'd been subjected to regular beatings
Instead of enduring injustices that gave him the chills
Like a less opulent bedroom than big brother Wills
While the great British public paid for his drug abuse bills
And the only fuckwitted tool to feign any sympathy
Was that smug twat who reads the news on ITV

Something else this prick does that gives me the hump
Is that sneering tone he adopts to talk about the Tories or Trump
And yes they're all grade one cunts but that isn't the point
Cos the world's saints and sinners aren't his to anoint
Impartiality's the very essence of a newsreader's job
So leave out all the spin, you self-worshipping knob
People hardly need excuses to stop watching the news
It's bad enough as it is without your personal views
But there the twat is, on our screens every day
When they circumcised him they threw the wrong bit away
There's no-one alive that I'd less rather be
Than that smug twat who reads the news on ITV

Old Man With Anger Management Issues Vs Automated Self-Service Checkout Machine In Marks And Spencers

This one is a particularly heartfelt rant. Getting old isn't great. Nothing works as well as it used to. Some things don't work at all. And you struggle to cope with developments that younger people deal with serenely – especially so-called technological advances. People sometimes mistake me for some sort of Tourettes afflicted nutter, and it happens more often in M&S than in any other environment. I swear at their machines very loudly and very often. Other customers sometimes look slightly afraid, but they have nothing to be worried about. I only ever perpetrate acts of violence on inanimate objects that can't fight back.

I'm sure part of my problem with these wretched things is due to my failure to follow the instructions – like "place basket here" - but it's always the machine that gets the blame. The assistants are invariably sympathetic, though maybe that's born of fear.

Even before I've scanned my first item I'm losing my rag
As the machine asks if I'm using my own bag
Which I am, and it's in the designated position
So why's it being treated with such suspicion?
"Unidentified item in the bagging area"
By the time the assistant arrives I'm going spare
It's just my shopping from elsewhere
So what's your problem?
If I put it on the floor I'd only forget it
And have to come back half an hour later to get it
'Cos I'm such a dozy sod.
You'll get an unidentified item next time, alright
And half your customers'll run off in fright
'Cos it'll be an industrial grade sledgehammer and it's going straight through that fucking machine

To increase my level of agitation
A shrill voice provokes pure aggravation
"Have you scanned your Sparks Card?"
You stuck-up, presumptuous, computerised bint
In Boots they ask me, "Do you have an advantage card?"
In Tesco it's, "Have you got a club card?"
So why does this automated voice of doom
Always automatically assume
That I've got a Sparks Card
As if it's required by law
Before I can even enter your store
And if I can't produce it on demand
Some flunkey'll grab me by the hand
And tell me to get orf his land
Well I've exercised my constitutional right not to have a Sparks Card
and you can't revoke it
So put that in your fucking pipe and smoke it

I take up the Indian meal offer - four items for a tenner
You'd think that'd be a no-brainer
But it proves to be a misguided notion
When the machine fails to spot that one of 'em's in the promotion
This gets me in a proper lather
And in no time there's a right palaver
As the assistant says the codes don't match
So we have to start again from scratch
And rescan not just the components of the special deal on the Indian meal
But every single item of shopping
It would have been so much quicker, slicker and better for my ticker
if I'd gone to a person in the first place
So why didn't I?
Because the queue was so long
And why was it so long?
Because so many people hate those fucking machines

Then, to my absolute terror
I realise I've made the schoolboy error
Of purchasing a box of cherry chocolate liqueurs
Which on account of their miniscule alcoholic content are classified as an age-restricted item
So why the hell do you refuse
To stack them alongside the booze
Instead of with the Jaffa Cakes
And the chocolate flakes
And the oatmeal bakes?
And why don't you bunch of witless cocks
Put the alcohol content on the box?
Because it's virtually fucking zero
You could binge eat sixteen boxes of these things, one a minute
And still be under the drink-drive limit
Not that I'd advocate eating sixteen boxes of chocolate liqueurs then going out for a spin
'Cos a state of nausea would soon kick in
And you'd throw up over the steering wheel
Which when you're doing seventy isn't ideal
But for now that's by the by
And an assistant comes to verify
That I appear to be over twenty-five years old
Not the greatest challenge to her powers of observation
And after a depressing lack of deliberation
She says no need for identification
Well thanks very much

Now I'm being told – really, how dare you -
I've removed an item from the bagging area
Well of course I have, because my bag's full and I need to start on a new one
What do you expect me to do, you electronic clown
Pile 'em all up till they come crashing down
Causing breakages galore
And spilling yogurt all over the floor
So your customers go arse over tit
And you end up being served with a writ
Demanding massive sums in compensation
For broken bones and dislocations
Which are all just figments of the imagination
Of fucking bastard ambulance chasers?

I almost forgot
I've got this promotional voucher
20% off breakfast cereal
But frankly that's just immaterial
'Cos there is not the faintest hope
This hapless machine will ever cope with that
Is it really worth creating a scene
And acting like a drama queen
To achieve a saving of 87 pence?
Well, yes it is actually
It's not the money, it's the principle
But once you start saying stuff like that
You realise that you're not just a bit of a prat
But in fact you're a complete wanker and shouldn't be allowed out in public
Just stay at home for evermore
And have it all delivered to your door
'Cos that's where all of this is heading
That's what all your staff are dreading
When you can close the doors to all your stores
And make everyone redundant
Well aren't you fucking clever

Don't Buy A Dyson

One of my most traumatic moments during lockdown was when our hoover broke down. I'm sure it was something to do with not cleaning the filters properly but I couldn't be arsed to investigate. And what with being incarcerated for month after month and unable to go out to pubs and restaurants we'd at least saved a few bob, so we decided to push the boat out and get ourselves a Dyson. Fucking posh bastards, eh?.

When it arrived a few days later, we unpacked it with eager anticipation and it was one of those moments when you know you've made it. How we looked forward to being able to invite the neighbours round so we could give them a serious dose of vacuum cleaner envy.

Well, it served us bloody well right. By the time we were allowed to have visitors we were so pissed off with this thing that we hid it out of sight, ashamed of having been duped, and duly punished for having ideas above our station. It's right up there as one of my all-time worst purchases. Absolute heap of shite. Don't let this happen to you.

They try to tell you their products are state of the art
You want my opinion, well where do I start?
When they release a new model you get killed in the rush
But you'd be better off with a dustpan and brush
It starts off like a dream, you think this isn't bad
But within half an hour you can tell you've been had
The motor keeps cutting out, there's a reduction in suction
And a serious design fault in this hoover's construction
It happens again and again, it's beyond problematic
Its airways clogged up like a chronic asthmatic
I'm left in a state of total disgust
Maybe me carpets have got the wrong kind of dust
Don't buy a Dyson

Their sales pitch is based on elitist psychology
"We developed this model using space-age technology"
That don't impress me much, you bollock-brained balloon
'Cos I don't want to go to the fucking moon
Something to keep me house tidy, that's all I ask
But these overpriced demmicks aren't up to the task
They're designed ergonomically for ease of manoeuvring
But you spend more time unblocking 'em than actually hoovering
They're like prog rock music, the hippies' delight
Elaborately constructed but fucking shite
And as for the inventors, those highly qualified boffins
I'll shoot 'em myself and pay for the coffins
Don't buy a Dyson

They market their products as being aspirational
To be honest, I'd settle for just operational
They call this a fantasy item, what are they talking about?
You want it to swallow, it spits everything out
It's time the great British public came to its senses
They're taking your money under false pretences
Stop buying these not fit for purpose devices
Exploiting their brand name to charge ludicrous prices
And who cares if their staff all end up being laid off
Cos they're the biggest con-artists since Bernie Madoff
After just a few months, it needs a new battery
Another shining example of incompetent twattery
So I go on the website, the price knocks me down flat
Seventy-five quid, you could buy a new hoover for that!
And I think I will

And it won't be a fucking Dyson

Rucksack Cunt

With every day that goes by, the proportion of the British public which seems to think it needs a rucksack in order to travel on public transport increases. And as soon as they strap it to their back they forget it's there. So thousands of passengers minding their own business get clubbed, battered and bruised by this bunch of irresponsible thoughtless clumsy shit-for-brains knobheads. They'll spill coffee onto your laptop. They'll smack you on the side of the head with the force of a Mike Tyson right hook. And they'll never apologise because as they rampage through the aisles of trains, buses and trams they remain blissfully oblivious to the mayhem they've caused. Or maybe they just don't care. What a bunch of cunts they are.

I need to grab a quick bite at the railway station
But all I get's exasperation
It's one of those places where you serve yourself
But I can't get anywhere near the shelf
For these dithering dickheads all in a flap
"Shall I have a quinoa salad or a hummus wrap?"
I only want a cheese sarny and a lemonade
But I can't fight through the canvas blockade
Erected by this fuckwitted army of rucksack cunts
So I have to leave empty-handed or I'll miss my train

We're queuing for the bus but right in front of us
Are these muppets who're twice their natural circumference
As the bus approaches one swings round
And clubs an old woman to the ground
He doesn't even notice and clambers aboard
With the rest of the overburdened horde
The seats are all taken but I'm ok, cos the sign on the landing
Says that there's room for twenty-six standing
No there fucking well isn't
There's room for just thirteen rucksack cunts
And I'm left standing on the pavement like a bloody lemon

They take public nuisance to another dimension
Are they going to a Quasimodo fan club convention?
'Cos there's loads of the bastards on this tram
All shaped like the Hunchback of Notre Dame
This letch gawped at one, who was scantily dressed
He couldn't take his eyes off her ample chest
He leered to his mate, "Cor, she's well stacked!"
But she's even bigger at the back
Cos she's a rucksack cunt
You'd get your recommended daily exercise just walking round her

They're ignorant, selfish and totally careless
With a staggering lack of spatial awareness
Do they think it just vanishes into thin air?
Just because you can't see it doesn't mean it's not there
Look at the size of that one, what a nightmare
He's only going to work, what the fuck's he got in there?
I tell him, "Be careful" and he reacts with outrage
Then he swivels and smacks me in the ribcage
I said, "You dozy bastard, you nearly cut me in half
Good job I'm not a fucking dwarf
You'd have had my head off!"
Rucksack cunt

Put it on the bloody floor!

Premature Christmas Twat

People say that Christmas starts earlier every year, but I'm not sure that's true. As a little boy I used to start getting excited around September, when the Christmas ads started on television and an enticing array of potential presents appeared in my mum's John Moores catalogue. I soon twigged that she hid my presents at the top of the wardrobe, but I kept up the pretence of believing in Santa Claus even though I knew it was a load of bollocks. As soon as she was out of the house, I'd stand on a chair and scavenge around, trying to find them. When I got a bit taller she started putting them into the loft, but that was no deterrent to a determined 32-year old armed with a pair of stepladders.

A few years ago I was in my local supermarket and noticed they had Christmas goodies on special offer. Mince pies, Christmas cakes, fancy chocolates and all that. It was mid-September. Out of curiosity I picked up a box of mince pies and clocked the sell-by date. November 5. They were selling Christmas produce which you were supposed to eat seven weeks before Christmas. This didn't feel right at all. I like a mince pie as much as the next man, but I don't want to be eating them in September. It's like having an Easter Egg in January. So I thought the best way to express my disgust would be to write a poem about it.

Christmas food's on sale at bargain prices
Mince pies, pannetone and stollen slices
Can't believe this guy's already bought 'em
It's barely even fucking autumn
He gets a quizzical look from the girl on the checkout
Do you honestly think these are gonna run out?
But he's saved a few bob, and he's feeling great
Till he notices the sell-by date
November the fifth, Guy Fawkes night
How the fuck can that be right?
By Christmas they'll be stale and old
With festering green spots of mould
She tried to warn you but you wouldn't be told
You premature Christmas twat

In shopping centres around the nation
The Christmas playlist's on rotation
Now the festive season's really begun
Here it is, merry Christmas, everybody's having fun
No we fucking well aren't...
It's pissing down, we're stone cold sober
It's still the middle of October
The cricket season's barely over
We're just not ready for Noddy Holder
Bellowing, "It's Christmas!!"
When it's not even fucking Halloween yet
Twelve days of Christmas are more than plenty
But in here we get more like a hundred and twenty
You premature Christmas twats

In this humdrum town it's a special night
When a big name comes to turn on the lights
But this year all the council could afford to enlist
Was a micro-celebrity plucked from the Z-list
He's a TV actor, on a minor scale
Appeared in two episodes of Emmerdale
He's vapid, vain and artificially tanned
But just for flicking a switch they paid him two grand
An offer like that, how could anyone resist
He took his loot down the wine bar to get royally pissed
He'd have been better off spending it on acting lessons
The lights come on to total indifference
You can hardly tell the fucking difference
Cos it's not even properly dark yet
You could at least wait until the clocks go back
You premature Christmas twats

Santa's been and gone, now it's Boxing Day
When folk go to watch their local team play
Take a bracing walk or hit the pub for a beer
Thanking God it's all over until next year
But next year's already on this twat's mind
As he wonders what bargains he can find
After all, there are only 364 shopping days to go
And you can never be too organised, you know
When you're the ultimate premature Christmas twat...

Sets his alarm and races to the store
Long before they open he's outside the door
The sale's on, with shelves full of hideous tat
But at these prices he doesn't care about that
Reduce stuff enough and he'll always buy some
He hoovers up cheap crap like a human Dyson[1]
Buys gift sets of toiletries that hundreds of shoppers refused
Most won't ever be opened, never mind used
And packs of miniature jams and marmalade
Every single one claiming to be home-made
He snaps up Christmas card packs at less than half price
60% off to be precise
To avoid embarrassment he has to hide 'em
But eleven months later he can't find 'em
...Try as he might
'Cos the penny-pinching sack of shite
Had tucked 'em away well out of sight
So now he doesn't feel so bright
But it just serves him bloody right
For being so fucking gnat's chuff tight
The premature Christmas twat

[1.] *This was written before I'd actually purchased a Dyson...*

NOSTALGIA

The older you get, the more things you've got to be nostalgic about. In general I'm a "never look back" sort of bloke – that way madness lies – but I do increasingly go through phases of listening solely to 60s and 70s music or watching vintage footy on YouTube. And I always enjoy it, even stuff that I didn't especially like at the time. That is properly weird. Are things really that shit these days that stuff you once thought was rubbish now seems really good? Or is it just how the brain works?

Funnily enough I never get nostalgic for the 80s, even though by then I was earning a living and generally having a nice time. Maybe that'll come later, but I rather suspect it won't.

Ashton Market (part one)

I was at a spoken word night in my home town of Ashton-under-Lyne when this chap read a lovely nostalgic poem. It was quite a simple piece but they're often the best and it really resonated with me. On the bus on the way home I started thinking about writing something in a similar vein.

So a couple of weeks later I went back to Ashton and spent some time just wandering round the market stalls, indoors and outdoors, trying to visualise what used to be there and revelling in the familiarity of some of the stallholder family names, unchanged even after all these years. Of course I bought some oven bottom muffins and Redman's salmon spread – the taste of my childhood during school holidays – and when I ate them later it transported me back instantly to having lunch on my gran's kitchen table. It's not just music that can take you back to a time and place.

I was amazed how many little details came flooding back during my meanderings and I ended up with enough material for two poems – one about when I was very little and one set in my teenage years. This is the first of them. It didn't turn out to be quite as nostalgic as I originally envisaged.

When you were little, the market was the place to be
And always the very first thing you'd see
Was a row of colourful fruit and veg stalls
Selling cauliflowers the size of beachballs
Prices on white card in black marker pen,
Satsumas three-ha'pence each or a shilling for ten
The words "special offer" were always rife,
You've never seen so many apostrophes in your life
We had such simple tastes back then
Carrots and cabbage left us all contented
Broccoli hadn't even been invented
If it had they'd never have been able to sell it
Certainly wouldn't have been able to spell it
And as for asparagus, well, good luck with that
There was no place for fancy exotic produce on Ashton Market

I'd often go with my gran
And if she stopped for a natter with Elsie or Lizzie
She'd let me go off and buy something fizzy
At a stall where cordial from a well-stocked bar
Stored in what looked like a specimen jar
Was topped up with soda water dispensed from a syphon
When the nice lady came to serve me I'd always tell her
"Please can I have a sarsaparilla"
For some an acquired taste
For others a never to be acquired taste
For a nine year-old the epitome of sophisticated taste
Edging even the mysterious Mancunian magnificence of Vimto into second place
In the hit parade of cool refreshments available on Ashton Market

When I got back to my gran her eyes were sometimes red from crying
As she'd spent yet another week desperately trying
To make ends meet
And on the days when she went in to pay the rent
I knew straight away this meant
That when the window cleaner came for his money
Or the insurance man came round
We'd have to stay silent and hit the ground
And pretend no-one was in
Keeping all the balls in the air was a hopeless task
A bit like a Tommy Cooper juggling act, but not quite so funny
Yet on the market she'd always find the money
To buy me an ice cream.
And even as a nipper I couldn't help but note
That all the women she talked to were in the same boat
A problem shared was a problem halved on Ashton Market

And on weekdays there were plenty to share it with
As the market ground became a kaleidoscope of colourful shopping trolleys with garish tartan patterns
Wheeled through the open spaces
By hunched figures with wizened, haggard faces
All desperately short of dough
All with nowhere else to go
Old before their time bodies broken by decades of manual labour
Futures with so very little to savour
Enduring, not enjoying, a retirement which would be short-lived
And miserable
And increasingly propped up by walking sticks and frames
And one by one these familiar faces would disappear
And instinctively you'd always fear
The worst
And usually you were right

But at least they'd had their three score years and ten
And maybe another five
But one day in 1965[1]
A woman, dark wigged over peroxide blonde hair
And a sinister man with an unsettling stare
Brought unspeakable evil to the market
Luring a young boy into their car
With the promise to take him to his door
But instead they buried him on Saddleworth moor.
And not one person then had the slightest understanding
Of why the hell they'd just abolished hanging
But in time most came to change their mind
Instant death, that's far too kind
Let them live every day with the memory of what they've done
They indeed might sleep, but they will never dream

And our mums and our dads
And our grans and our grandads
And our aunts and our uncles
And our friends and our neighbours
Would hammer home the mortal dangers
Of ever accepting lifts from strangers
So ingrained did this mantra become
So often did we hear them say it
That even now we still obey it
And if a driver pulls over to ask the way
Or someone stops us for a light
Our instinct's to step back, as if in fright
Our lack of faith in human nature cemented at such a young age
These days they call it being streetwise
But really wouldn't it be nice
To trust people a little bit more?
But we never forget that we were the lucky ones
Because even when the sun shines through
And the sky's an unbroken sea of blue
There's a corner shrouded in permanent darkness
On Ashton Market

> [1.] Bit of poetic license here. John Kilbride was actually abducted from the market in 1963, but details of what had happened to him didn't emerge until two years later, and that's the bit that I remember vividly. I can still feel the chill which descended on our estate, where we youngsters had always enjoyed the freedom to come and go as we pleased, on-one ever imagining that such evil was amongst us. At a stroke we all became far more closely supervised by our families.

Maine Road Matchday '69

This is a poem about being a twelve year-old boy who absolutely hated school and lived for Saturday afternoons. It's about the sights, sounds and smells of Maine Road. I went to my first game there in 1967, although it was another couple of years before I was allowed to start going regularly. My most vivid recollections of watching football come from this and the following two or three years.

Although the stadium is long gone, the memories will always remain, which I suppose shows how important football – and City – were to me at the time. They still are, but the difference these days is that by the time I've walked back home from the Etihad, I'm already struggling to remember who scored the goals. Though, to be fair, that's often because there've been so many of them...

A week at school wished away
Until at last it's Saturday
Matchday
Maine Road matchday
Solemn commitment to worried mum
"I'll be ok, I'm meeting a schoolchum"
Usually a lie, sometimes true
Most times I don't, now and then I do

Bus to Piccadilly, the 219
Passing by the Courtaulds sign
Then straight to Lewis's department store
TV showroom, fourth floor
An array of tellies for sale or for rent
A small crowd gathers, all male, one intent
To watch football previews - in colour! A proper treat
Then through the gardens to Aytoun Street
For the football special, a red Routemaster
Though some days you could walk it faster

Unshaven men with unwashed hands
Wait for custom at burger stands
Stained white overalls define their style
Not seen Persil for quite a while
Grubby nails on nicotine fingers
Haven for germs to thrive and linger
Burgers stacked in a tepid lake
Laced with fag ash, almost opaque
Not exactly items to savour
Like soggy cardboard, with slightly less flavour
Vegans hadn't been invented yet
But if they had you can bet
They could have dined here safely
(Apart from the obligatory tummy upset)

Floodlight pylons, an arresting sight
Frame Moss Side drizzle in vibrant light
Fumble in pocket for half a crown
Through creaking turnstiles, put the money down
Programme seller, refreshment stand
Last few coppers clasped in hand
Flat-capped men clutch cups of Bovril
Repulsive odour fills the nostrils
Not a drink for little boys
Kia-Ora orange, that's my choice
Money less than wisely spent
Real fruit content - zero percent

Now time to spend another penny
But so few facilities for so many
Cascading rivers of metabolised booze
Fag ends hurtling along like canoes
Shooting the rapids, though this water's not white
The stench unspeakable, that can't be right
Is this what it's like in a man's world?

All set to ascend the stairway to heaven
To watch my heroes, one to eleven
Hordes of eager trampling feet
Pound on steps of crumbling concrete
Disintegration into rubble
Can only mean impending trouble
Paint peels on rusting railings
Glaring health and safety failings
Never properly put to the test
Fingers crossed and hope for the best
Ibrox, two years on, sixty-six will die
There, but for the grace of God, go I

Out come the teams to do their worst
Opponents first, always opponents first
"Bring on the champions," the Kippax boys roar
Even though we're not champions any more
But we are still pretty damn good
Even on a pitch awash with mud
No names on the back of those shirts of sky blue
But I don't even need numbers to tell who's who
Bell's athletic, imperious stride,
Lee chest out, bursting with pride,
Young floating with balletic grace
Book's hunched gait and unlikely pace
I gaze out in awe, mesmerised
Precious images forever prized

Crowd disturbance, a sudden buzz
Rival fans on the loose, here come the fuzz
For those around me a huge distraction
But my eyes stay firmly on the action
People lean across for a better view
And I just think, "What's wrong with you?"
Our games aren't on telly, well hardly ever
So blink and you'll have missed it forever
Giving morons the oxygen of attention
Even then well beyond my comprehension

Final whistle, don't see me for dust
Sprinting away to run for the bus
At speed through dithering crowds I go
Sit next to someone with a radio
Final scores and reports from familiar voices
If United have lost the whole bus rejoices
At last Piccadilly, will the Pinks have arrived?
Was that first goal offside? Will they say Franny dived?

Read the Pink on the bus, cover to cover
Even the letters page, why do these people bother?
Relentless banality, always the same
From armchair experts, never been to a game

Walk home from the bus station, knock at the door
Mum's there to meet me, she knows the score
Mood wholly dependent on how well we've done
Tea always tastes much better if we've won
Then *The Avengers* and *Match of the Day*
Followed by Sunday, grisly Sunday
The looming grim spectre of school on Monday
But Wednesday evening we're at home again
Another trip to Maine Road's my week's only aim
Planting the seeds, night after night
"Please mum, it'll be alright
Some lads from school are going..."

Reasons To Be Nostalgic, part 1

This poem takes us into the 1970s, by far my favourite decade. It embraced the teenage and university years, some great City teams, and what remains my favourite music of all time. My God there was some desperately grim stuff going on as well, but let's forget about that and celebrate some of the things really worth celebrating. And some which just happened to be around at the time.

This was inspired – if that's the right word - by Ian Dury's Reasons To Be Cheerful part 3, essentially a list poem set to music. This is a list poem not set to music, though if anyone can conjure up something appropriate I'd love to give it a go!

The 1970s were grisly, they say
A decade of darkness and decay
Maybe that's true, but on reflection
There's lots to remember with real affection

Spangles, Black Jacks, Opal Fruits
Platform shoes and bovver boots
Lemon puffs and Jammie Dodgers
Lulu, Cilla and Clodagh Rodgers
Stan and Hilda, Rita and Mavis
World of Sport with Dickie Davies
Henry Cooper, the great smell of Brut
Football Monthly, Goal! and Shoot!
Tony the Tiger, the Milky Bar Kid
A night on the town for a couple of quid
Walnut whips, sherbet dips
Blackpool illuminations trips
Chimpanzees and PG Tips

Used car salesmen, "One careful owner"
Manuel, he's from Barcelona
Woodchip, flock and anaglypta
Alice Cooper's boa constrictor
Poly Styrene, X-Ray Spex
Emmanuelle and the Joy of Sex
Tony Curtis with Roger Moore
Larry Grayson, "Shut that door"
Kenny Lynch and Acker Bilk
Black Tower, Blue Nun and Liebfraumilch
Hillman Imp and Ford Cortina
Confessions of a Window Cleaner
Don't Cry For Me, Argentina

Grease, Hair and Oh! Calcutta!
Stork margarine, can you tell it's not butter?
Dick Dastardly and Wacky Races
The glory days of Belle Vue Aces
Space Hoppers, Raleigh Choppers
Donny Osmond teenyboppers
Bryan Ferry's white tuxedo
Budgie smugglers made by Speedo
Rocket lollies and strawberry Mivvis
Green Shield stamps and Coop divis
Good old Woollies pick'n'mix
Cheese and pineapple on cocktail sticks
Tommy Cooper's magic tricks

John Noakes and Peter Purves
Park Drive, Woodbine, Senior Service
Mary Peters, golden girl
Anthea Redfern – "give us a twirl"
Blackforest gateau, Arctic Roll
Glam rock, punk and northern soul
Jubilee parties in the streets
Avocado bathroom suites
Data stored on microfiche
Real men, who wouldn't dare eat quiche
Pans People, Legs and Co
Pot Black with Whispering Ted Lowe
Eric and Ernie's Christmas show

Walls Neapolitan, raspberry ripple
The Daily Express, where you never saw a nipple
Tobacco adverts deemed unlawful
But not Dick Emery – "ooh, you are awful"
Connors thrashed by Arthur Ashe
Cup a Soup and Cadbury's Smash
School dinners, like it or lump it
Joan Bakewell, the thinking man's crumpet
Cup final crowds with home-made banners
Haystacks, Daddy and Mick McManus
Polyester replacing cotton
Bill Grundy goading Johnny Rotten
And some folk who are best forgotten

These days you never see their faces
But at least the 70s had some saving graces
Whereas the 1980s, well, they really were shit…

Ashton Market (part two)

Staying in the 1970s, this second Ashton market poem embraces my teenage years and again some memories that if you weren't around in the era then they probably won't mean very much.

You still see tripe on sale at stalls inside the market, and it looks as hideously unappetising as it always did, but I've not come across elder for many a decade. I can't say I miss it. I never actually tasted it but just the sight of it made my stomach churn.

Piled high on Saturday's trestle tables
Were coats with imitation branded labels
In synthetic fibres from abroad
But these were all we could afford
A famous blue raincoat, wouldn't that be nice
But on sale here at half the price
Were veritable stacks and stacks
Of infamous black anoraks

Imported from lands impossibly distant
These items were allegedly weather-resistant
Though it was never quite clear exactly what weather they were built to resist.
If you pushed the boat out and paid top dollar
The deluxe models had hoods tucked into the collar
Which you'd put to use on rainy days
But by the time you got back to your place
Your hair would be matted to your face
And water would seep inside your coat
And you'd be soaked from your waist right up to your throat
And as you wrung your t-shirt out to dry
Your mum would ask you why oh why
Did you buy yet another duff item from Ashton Market?

The cheapest way to fill your belly
Was to visit what posh folk now call a deli
Where alongside meat pies of every type
Was a tray bearing great big slabs of tripe
And elder, a sickly shade of beige
You wouldn't call it all the rage
In fact the only person you ever saw eat it was your grandad
He'd douse it with Sarsons to obliterate the taste
And you'd watch him wolf it down in haste
And think, "How the hell could anyone eat that?"

But it'll come back in fashion, just wait and see
In a wonderful new recipe
Created by Heston Blumental
And served in portions ever so small
Which cost as much as a brand new telly
But you won't regret a single penny
Spent on sampling the unique flavour sensation of this classic British dish
Yeah, right
But then who'd ever have thought people would eat raw fish?
Well, not here they don't
Sushi bars are still thin on the ground on Ashton Market

There were hardware stalls with DIY devices
And batteries at knockdown prices
Which for bargain hunters seemed highly pleasing
But these things were dirt cheap for a reason
If Duracell batteries were long life, the ones you'd just bought were destined for cot death
You'd get home and put 'em in your radio
To listen to the Kenny Everett show
And if City were away and you couldn't go
They'd last through the commentary in the afternoon
But they'd run out of juice all too soon
And never survive long enough
To hear Alan Freeman, dear old Fluff

Say, "Greetings, pop-pickers" at tea-time on Sunday
So you'd have to wait till school on Monday
To find out what was this week's number one
You got what you paid for on Ashton Market

For cool adolescents who were on the ball
The main attraction was the second-hand record stall
Where for 25 pence it was worth the risk
Of buying an ex-jukebox disc
Though to this very day I've no idea why
I bought Bob Marley's *No Woman No Cry*
I didn't even have a record player at the time, and I couldn't stand reggae
At least that was until the day
I heard *White Man In Hammersmith Palais*

The only thing that I can guess
Is I was influenced by the music press
Cos when the NME heard Marley sing
They said he'd be the next big thing
And yes, Bob will never be forgotten
But *my* next big thing was Johnny Rotten
Shaking Britain's youth out of its slumber
With an understated little number
Called *Anarchy In The UK*
The soundtrack to those golden years
Of jumpers for goalposts and underage beers
Is etched in grooves bought on Ashton Market

Go there now and its different for sure
Though still hardly a hotbed of *haute couture*
The styles aren't ever up to the minute
But to go out of fashion you firstly need to be in it
It got burned down, but it got up again
You ain't ever gonna keep it down
And still the proud centrepiece of this town
Is Ashton Market

HEROES AND VILLAINS

I've always had heroes and still do. Mainly in sport and music, which have been my main passions ever since I was little. I've picked three of many for this section. But of course, we live in a world where villains are far more plentiful than heroes, and for baddies I was absolutely spoilt for choice. It's so much easier to be nasty than nice; well, it is for me anyway, although I do try to reserve it for those who deserve it. (Christ, I'm rhyming in the introductions now, get a fucking grip...) And the three villains selected here are well worthy of anyone's contempt...

Frank

My comedy hero is Frank Sidebottom. All art forms can be polarising, and maybe none more so than comedy. And Frank was comedy marmite. If you got him, if you were on his wavelength, you thought he was the funniest thing ever; if you didn't, you'd just stand and watch and think "what the hell is funny about that?" There wasn't much middle ground.

I have wonderful memories of going to Frank's gigs, many of which have thankfully been preserved on YouTube, along with myriad TV clips. When his creator Chris Sievey died in 2010, it was absolutely one of those moments where you remember exactly where you were when you heard the news. Most deaths of people whose work you've enjoyed sadden you but don't affect your daily life, in my case because usually they're sportsmen who long since stopped playing or rock stars who seldom if ever tour or produce new music. But this was different, because Frank once again seemed to be gigging almost continuously and I'd go to see him as often as I possibly could. And the fact that I'd got to know Chris a bit over the previous couple of years made it hit so much harder.

Ten years on, and Chris's friend and collaborator Dave Arnold was putting together a tribute show and asked me to write a piece about Frank. If you're not familiar with the great man's work then most of the references will be absolutely meaningless. But if you know, you know…

Ten years have passed since that awful day
When Chris and Frank both passed away
Real life and fantasy departed together
And in these grim times they're missed more than ever

Those classic gigs with his puppet pals
Playing Freddie Mercury[1] and heavy metal[2]
And his Beatles renditions were better by far
Than those with McCartney on bass[3] guitar

The *Match of the Day* years saw Frank in his prime
His big shorts were way ahead of their time
But now that she's lost her big blue eyed son
I hope someone's been doing the shopping for his mum

There was panic on the streets of Timperley, he said
But now there's a fantastic statue instead
The Being Frank film, the Bobbins exhibition
Such bittersweet but richly deserved recognition

Without Frank there's much less fun in our lives
But work of such brilliance will always survive
At least the world's now aware of the genius of Chris
He'd always craved fame – and now, too late, it's his

Every day at precisely 11.37
Frank looks down from his fantastic shed, in heaven
He sees Little Frank tucked up in his cardboard bed
But still no sign of Little Denise's head[4]

1. *Pronounced Mer – CURE – ee*
2. *Pronounced m'TAL*
3. *Pronounced to rhyme with gas*
4. *Little Denise was created as Little Frank's girlfriend but her head was stolen at a gig in the late 1980s and, despite nationwide appeals, has never been seen since. Rather than create a new head, Frank continued to utilise a Little Denise body in his act, allowing Little Frank to continue his charmingly platonic relationship with a headless cardboard girlfriend.*

   Like I said, you either get this stuff or you don't...

Spanish Dave

I never imagined that City would ever have a player who could supersede Colin Bell as my all-time favourite, but David Silva managed it. He had this almost imperceptible quality of being able to bring the ball under his spell more quickly than anyone else, and also seemed to carry a 360-degree picture of where everything was around him. These attributes so often allowed him to provide his teammates with that extra fraction of time and space to do their thing, thereby making them better players as well. The way he played and moved embodied the very essence of why it's called the beautiful game.

Sadly, his ten-year stay ended during Covid times, denying City fans the opportunity to give him the send-off he deserved, but the statue outside the Etihad serves as a permanent reminder of this master craftsman, the most aesthetically pleasing of footballers.

So quiet on his debut, has he got what it takes?
He'll need building up, better feed him on steak
They said, "24 million, is that some kind of joke
What use will he be on a wet night at Stoke?"

But in no time at all, we could see what we'd got
Was a player who might be the best of the lot
Killer through balls, balletic pirouettes
A first touch to die for, as good as it gets

Weaving this way and that, with effortless grace
A supernatural ability to find pockets of space
Flicks, tricks and dummies, a talent supreme
But only ever employed for the good of the team

Clatter into his ankles, smash him to the floor
He'll just dust himself down and come back for more
Two men at his back but he still wants the ball
Only the bravest play with no fear at all

Like Colin the King, so humble and shy
At his best in the derbies, he made those reds cry
Six wins at Old Trafford, no Blue's ever had more
And the pass of a lifetime for Edin to bring up THAT score

Ten glorious years, so many pots won
With Zaba and Yaya, Vinny and Kun
Now those pundits who'd dissed him all say the same
If you don't love this guy then you don't love the game
A privilege to watch, a joy to behold
To be treasured forever, our Silva's pure gold

Five Years

David Bowie is another where I'll always remember where I was when I heard of his passing. It was such a shock. He was without doubt the most influential artist of my lifetime. His unique status was summed up perfectly by an ad around the time that the punks were ripping up the musical landscape, denouncing pretty much everything that had gone before. "There's new wave, there's old wave...and there's David Bowie". All the great bands of that era, and almost everything of interest that came afterwards, have acknowledged their debt to Bowie.

After he died it occurred to me that for all the artists that I've come to know and love, I still play Bowie's stuff more often than anyone else's. This poem references many of my favourite albums and songs of his and is titled after a track from Ziggy Stardust. It was originally written to mark the fifth anniversary of his death but when I wheel it out each January I just add another year.

Five years, that's all it's been
So many reflections on things we'd seen
Like that night in the summer of '72
I had to phone someone so I picked on you
Us kids thought, "Wow", parents cowered in fright
Thank God most tellies were just black and white
The papers wanted to know whose shirts you wore
And your dresses and make-up and jumpsuits galore
Even those you offended couldn't help glancing
Does he mean it, John, or is he only dancing?

Ziggy, Aladdin and Halloween Jack
You made 'em, we played 'em, then they never came back
A mass of cocaine, a mess on *Soul Train*
But you stunned us again with another new look
Falling to earth with the Thin White Duke

Pallid ghostly white skin, impossibly thin
Crossing from Station to Station, next stop Berlin
Where the music created with Eno then Fripp
Was startling and radical and incredibly hip
Your Low was a high, then the sight of the wall
Inspired the most memorable anthem of all

Punk demolished a musical landscape so grey
Prog rock and metal had had their day
For those dinosaurs, the tills stopped ringing
But you stayed in fashion, your boys kept swinging
Picking up new influences like a vulture
You cemented yourself in popular culture
Lightning flash souvenirs, millions shifted
"Heroes" always the soundtrack to trophies being lifted
Ashes to Ashes and Life on Mars
Turned Glenister, Hawes and Simm into stars
David Bowie Is, an inspired exhibition
A mesmeric immersion in sound and vision
But then David Bowie was…

So sudden the news on that fateful day
Then we found out you'd planned it that way
"Look up here, I'm in heaven" made the world stand still
Hardly anyone knew you'd even been ill
A consummate showman to the final breath
Even making an art form out of your death

Five years, that's all it's been
So much written heard and seen
An inspiration to everyone who tries to create
Don't rest on your laurels, that's how you stagnate
Never be frightened to try something new
You'll amaze yourself with what you can do

Don't we all wonder sometimes…

The Ballad Of Desperate Don

This is the only poem I've so far performed with a musical backing track. Well, "performed" is over-egging it a bit, as it's only ever been inflicted on participants at zoom spoken word nights, from the sanctuary of my study at home.

I stuck a cutout Donald Trump head onto one of my Little Frank bodies and waved it about a bit in front of the laptop camera, while hiding under my desk. I then blasted out the backing track to The Ting Tings' That's Not My Name while shouting out my adapted lyrics in the style of Frank Sidebottom's majestic cover version – "they call me Sidey, they call me big head, they call me pumpkin head..."

This wasn't exactly animation at its most sophisticated but I really enjoyed doing it. I'd love to do it live, as no doubt we'll be hearing more from Desperate Don as he fights to avoid a custodial sentence or, God forbid, seeks re-election but I still haven't quite worked out how to deliver it. Friends sometimes ask me why I have absolutely zero appetite to revisit the USA. "They elected Donald Trump" is a pretty good starting point.

They call me shithead
They call me fuckwit
They call me bollockbrain
They call me twatface

That's not my name, no
That's not my name, no
That's not my name, no
That's not my name

They call me racist
They call me sexist
They call me homophobe
They call me bigot

They call me bully
They call me tyrant
They call me rapist
They call me terrorist

They call me bellend
They call me narcissist
They call me shameful
Enemy of democracy

That's not my name, no
That's not my name, no
That's not my name, no
That's not my name

They call you powerful
They call you mighty
They call you POTUS
Mr President

That's not your name, no
That's not your name, no
That's not your name, no
That's not your name, no

Now just fuck off and don't come back

He's Boris

I've never had the slightest interest in politics, concluding at an early age that, whatever their affiliation, every single politician is consumed by self-interest and ambition, and that any pretence of caring for the people they represent comes from a place of zero sincerity. A mate of mine said to me, "Anyone who puts themselves forward to be a politician should immediately be disqualified from becoming one" and I think that sums up how I feel as well.

Worse still, we're slowly lurching towards the circus that is the USA, where politics is more reality TV than something to be taken seriously. And naturally attracts candidates to match. Watching some of the Brexit debate, where protagonists on both sides wilfully fed flagrant lies every night to the viewing public, just confirmed that the whole thing was just a game. And things reached a nadir when Boris Johnson became Prime Minister.

If you were on holiday during the Johnson era and the locals discovered where you came from, they'd react half with mockery, half with pity. This is what having a total dickhead in charge does for your international reputation. It made you ashamed to be British. I wrote this while Boris was embroiled in his final, futile, battle to cling to power.

Only in America, we all said about Trump
Then we ended up with our very own bollock-brained lump
Cos as prize dickheads go they don't come any better
If you called him a banker you'd be out by one letter
His image consultant said "let your hair grow"
But then the cunt looked like a fucking scarecrow
He's the very antithesis of a national treasure
The only BJ that never brings any pleasure
A British prime minister? In a bizarre work of fiction
Where being a bumbling twat's part of the job description
But his craving for power's an all-consuming addiction
He's Boris

There's no middle ground, you either loathe him or hate him
For the sake of humanity can't someone castrate him
He owns up to eight kids with three different mothers
But the rumours persist about quite a few others
'Cos this slobbering sex-crazed repulsive lardbucket
Lives his life by the mantra of "if it moves, fuck it"
His cheating is serial, his lying habitual
Does shagging the nanny form part of his daily ritual?
His alley-cat morals are indefensible
His attraction to women incomprehensible
Even for a Tory he's reprehensible
He's Boris

No shame, no humility, no compassion, no grace
While we suffered he got pissed and stuffed cake in his face
His don't give a toss leadership went on at full throttle
Every cabinet meeting was bring your own bottle
He gives a sly smirk as the Ukraine war rages
"Excellent work Vladimir, it keeps me off the front pages"
His "I'm being sincere" act shows no sign of improving
You can tell when he's lying cos his lips are moving
Clings to power like a drowning man clutching a raft
Why leave now, with so many more poor bastards to shaft
Do the right thing and resign, don't be so fucking daft
He's Boris

But then at last came the camel's back-breaking straw
Which even his grovelling cronies thought was one lie too far
He appointed a sleazy pathetic no-hoper
Well aware the sad twat was a notorious groper
Still he tried to hang on, they'll have drag him out screaming
Why can't he go now, what the fuck is he scheming?
I'll say this for the twat, he's certainly no quitter
The worst leader we've ever had? Well, since Gary Glitter...
So good riddance at last to this hapless buffoon
The human equivalent of a hot air balloon
And if he ever comes back it'll be way too soon
He's Boris

Neville

One of the natural traits of committed football supporters is that we often derive more pleasure from the failures of our rivals than we do from our own club's successes. This is definitely not healthy, but it's what we do.

And what we also do is develop hate figures. And when you've been following a team for well over fifty years, and you're blessed with a brutally vindictive nature, then your list of hate figures starts to resemble a telephone directory. The competition is fierce, but if I had to pick one person to be at the very top of my own list, it would be Gary Neville. I hated him as a player – what City fan didn't? – but I find him even more insufferable as a pundit and increasingly, unbelievably, a "celebrity".

I do have a burgeoning selection of tales to tell of my encounters with the boy Neville but that, literally, is another story. In the meantime, this poem is based unashamedly on John Cooper Clarke's classic late-70s insult-fest "Twat". I didn't actually start writing it with Neville in mind but then I slotted in a couple of tailored verses to go with the "one size fits all" torrent of abuse I'd already got.

His parents met over a parking ticket on a double yellow line
They said it was a perfect match, Cruella De Vil meets Frankenstein

When he was born, his gruesome features made the midwife chunder
No-one could bear to look at him, not even Stevie Wonder

His mother sent him out to play, come rain, or hail or snow
She hoped he'd finally get the hint, and find somewhere else to go

He begged to be let back inside, saying, "Mum, I'm freezing cold"
But that door wouldn't open till she'd located her blindfold

She took him to a plastic surgeon, he said "I'm not a miracle worker!
Shame he wasn't born a girl, you could have dressed him in a burqa"

He tried to get a summer job, but couldn't find any takers
So he ended up a model for a firm of gargoyle makers

When his mates were all out on the pull, where was he to be seen?
In his bedroom with a blow-up doll and a jar of Vaseline

He thought he'd have a chance with one of Rooney's cast-off hags
But even they won't let him near unless he wears three paper bags

Daleks hid behind the sofa whenever they saw his face
They feared this vile mutation could wipe them out without a trace

He walks into a crowded bar, it empties double quick
A fleeting glimpse of that moustache makes grown men physically sick

His face looks like his playground scraps were all against Joe Frazier
He's a one-man vindication of the case for euthanasia

We all know that looks don't matter, 'cos personality comes first
But he's such a loathsome scumbag this makes things even worse

He truly is repulsive, top to bottom, back to front
They can't find a good word for him, but I can – Neville

LOCKDOWN

A few years on and it's difficult to reconcile what we all lived through. Just the annual reminders to get our top up jabs are all that remain for those of us lucky enough to have come through the pandemic completely unscathed. There are times when it feels like it never actually happened.

But of course it did happen, bringing with it the zoom quizzes, the remote working, the supermarket home deliveries, the daily walks embracing areas never previously visited even though we'd lived in the vicinity for donkey's years and, as restrictions were released, the recognition that little things we'd previously taken for granted were actually pretty wonderful.

We had to find new ways to keep ourselves entertained and in spoken word world, one of the most important - and most enjoyable - was the emergence of zoom spoken word nights. Most of our other activities had fallen by the wayside, but here we could continue to indulge our passion for writing and performing, while keeping in touch with an even broader community than was possible in the real world. These gave us something to look forward to rather than sitting around watching telly, YouTube and the like. So heartfelt thanks to all those who made the effort to put these events on. (See *Acknowledgements* later.) It might be a bit overdramatic to call them life-savers, but they were certainly vitally important in helping us stay sane.

I always said I wouldn't write about lockdown, because so many others were doing it far better than I ever could, but in the end I relented largely because there was so little else going on and I'd run out of things to rant about.

Wear A Mask, You Selfish...Person

I was definitely at the cautious end of the spectrum when Covid emerged, while accepting, to a point, that others might take a more relaxed view. What I didn't appreciate, however, was the lack of consideration and respect for those of us who were genuinely concerned for our own welfare and that of others, especially in those early pre-vaccine days.

This poem takes the form of a conversation between a decent human being and a dickhead. For the avoidance of doubt, the dickhead's contributions are in italics...

Would customers kindly wear a mask
You wouldn't think that's a lot to ask
Can it really be all that much bother
To look after yourself and look after each other?
Apparently so

*You can't make me wear one of these things
My civil liberties are being infringed!*

Don't you make me bloody cringe
I've never heard anyone spout such drivel
If you want liberties just try being civil

You see the mask-up sign, you sneer and scoff
Without a care you splutter and cough
You deserve to have your bits cut off
Strutting around feeling invincible
Not giving a toss as a matter of principle
Can't you see that old lady looking so nervous
Wondering if she dare touch that surface
And wishing they'd bring back national service

I know there've been some tragic stories
But it's all the fault of those bastard Tories
Their leadership has been a farce
Signs of compassion are bloody sparse
So why the hell should I be arsed?

I take your point but that's no defence
For a total lack of common sense
We all know Boris is a grade one cock
His cronies just a laughing stock
Ballsing it up around the clock
Breaking their own rules, well there's a shock
But put aside your politics please
Cos governments don't spread this disease
People do
People like me - and people like you

But a few weeks ago they said masks were no use
Now if I don't wear one I get dog's abuse

Oh come on, they've never known what they're doing
From day one there's been disaster brewing
Mixed messages, U-turns, total confusion
Suggestions of competence just an illusion
But even if their guidance had been a *tour de force*
You'd still ignore it as a matter of course
Because let's be honest, that's what you do
Everything is you you you

I don't know why you're so het up really
Cos the whole thing's just a conspiracy theory
Concocted as a timely distraction
To neutralise dissatisfaction
At the lack of decisive Brexit action

Mate, you're living in a parallel universe
Like Donald Trump but even worse
Where the moon's made of cheese, the earth is flat
Piers Morgan isn't really a twat
Elvis is alive, well fancy that
Living in a Salford council flat
Where Michael Jackson pops round for a chat
Honestly, what are you lot like
Who wouldn't want Boris to get on his bike
But you'd replace him with David Icke

You're the people we need to confront
Cos you don't give a damn, and let's be blunt
I've seen folk with more empathy in the National Front
So just wear a mask, you selfish…person

Relentless

Covid was grim for everyone, but for some more than others. I definitely suffered far less than most. When I did test positive I had no symptoms whatsoever, and no-one close to me got seriously ill. And when you spend a lot of your time writing, you're used to being on your own, so the disruption to my daily routine wasn't anywhere near as great as for most other people.

But there's a difference between choosing to be on your own and having it forced on you, and it was the lack of variety, the Groundhog Day nature of living through lockdown, that eventually got to me, the fact that I couldn't go out even if I wanted to. I thought that a poem with a simple repetitive rhyming structure would best capture that feeling of being trapped day after day after day.

Peering through the windowpane
At gloomy skies and pouring rain
Me holiday plans are down the drain
What I'd give to get onto a plane
Or even on a bloody train
But the powers that be have made it plain
From travelling we must abstain
So indoors we must all remain
Living life in the very slow lane

This incarceration's inhumane
Life's so relentlessly mundane
We're not allowed to entertain
So we watch the telly yet again
Where with utterances so inane
Ministers pile on the pain
Creatives treated with disdain
"What's your problem? Just retrain!"
Next election you'll be slain

Those experts exercise your brain
With their educational campaign
We watch in fear as they explain
How the virus lives on cellophane
From their evidence they ascertain
The infection rate's now on the wane
But can't eradicate it, just contain
And pray that vaccines break this chain

This sacrifice mustn't be in vain
Can't face this cycle yet again
So though it goes against the grain
And causes grievous mental strain
From fun and frolics we must refrain
It's really pointless to complain
So much to lose, so little to gain
So let's try to keep each other sane
Until the day they finally deign
To let us out to drink Champagne
Or a French red from some posh domaine
Or a nice Rioja from sunny Spain
Or a prosecco or a Guinness or a pint of real ale
Or a gin and tonic or a trendy cocktail
Or a San Miguel or a Peroni or a Coors Light
Or a cheap and nasty buy two glasses get the rest of the bottle free house white
Or a paintstripper brandy or a half of shandy
Or a bottle of sickly sweet artificially flavoured cider with more E-numbers than you can shake a stick at
Or a pint of warm gassy beer in a plastic glass
Anything really, anything at all
Please just let us out!

Amazing

After months of incarceration, and the depressing sight of cafes, pubs and restaurants being closed for business – some never to re-open – there came a phase where we were allowed to eat and drink al fresco. On the first day this concession was granted it was bloody freezing but nothing was going to stop us. It's the first time I've ever eaten out wearing gloves.

Shortly afterwards we were allowed inside – masked up, socially distanced and sanitised – and it felt like another huge step forward. Like many people, I seem to be far more productive when I'm sitting in a café than when I'm working at home. But on this particular day I was barely productive at all, just happy to be reacquainting myself with low scale social interaction.

It somehow didn't seem right to try to put this into rhyming verse, so I had a go at describing it like a "proper" poet might have done. I read it once over zoom but didn't really enjoy it – I felt a bit lost without the reassuring rhythm of rhyme. Maybe it works a bit better on the page.

Coffee shops are open again
A welcome change of scene
I venture out, excitedly
For a small taste of how life used to be
Well, almost

Table service only
Fully sanitised
A pleasant young lady brings the menu for my perusal
Every hot beverage known to man
And some unknown, at least to this man
But she's wasting her time
I know what I want
Hipster-friendly temptations abound
But I'm not a man for turning

"Just a black coffee, please"
She looks at me and smiles
"Amazing!"
Amazing
Man goes into coffee shop and orders cup of coffee
Amazing

I know people these days are prone to hyperbole
But come on
Could I have asked for anything more ordinary?
Maybe it's the very fact that I ordered something so startlingly humdrum that she finds amazing
Maybe that's not what people do in here
Maybe you're supposed to have a cappuccino or a cortado or a macchiato or a mocha or a latte or a mocha latte
Or even a hot chocolate with whipped cream and syrup and marshmallows and a chocolate flake
Jesus Christ are they trying to kill people?
Maybe she's amazed that an old geezer like me can breeze into this trendy joint and have the gall, the temerity, the audacity to request such a mundane drink when so many more exotic, more exciting, more happening, more thoroughly modern beverages are there for the taking
Maybe that's it
Maybe she thinks, "Wow! This guy's got some serious balls
Waltzing in here utterly brazen
Unkempt and unshaven
With his mangy t-shirt and his scruffy tracksuit bottoms
And his ancient trainers and his battered old laptop
And ordering just a black coffee"
Amazing

She returns to my table
"Did you want milk?"
I had rather hoped
And indeed expected
That my request for a black coffee
Might have provided sufficient clarity as to the extent of my dairy product requirement
But she's polite and smiley and welcoming, so the last thing I want to do is be a smartarse
"No, black will be fine thanks"

I haven't got a hangover
I always take my coffee black
I don't like milk
I'm not lactose intolerant
Just fucking intolerant
Especially of milk
Skimmed milk, semi-skimmed milk
Not skimmed in any shape or form milk
Oat milk, goat milk, Mongolian throat milk
Coconut milk, soy milk, almond milk, cashew milk, peanut milk, any kind of nut milk
Anything but milk
I pour orange juice over my breakfast cereal, that's how much I don't like milk
And anyway, do I look like the sort of bloke who puts milk in his coffee?
When I walked in, did she glance at me and think "this guy looks like a proper cappuccino merchant"
I hope not
Although I must admit that I do like a nice peppermint tea,
And I'm quite partial to a touch of the old lemon and ginger as well
But please keep that to yourselves, I've got a reputation to maintain

My coffee arrives
Black
No milk
I linger over it as I continue to edit some poem or story or chapter or whatever it is I'm playing about with today
People come and people go, with their fancy drinks and fancy food
Usually incorporating a high avocado content
But I'm not tempted
To be honest I didn't even really want a coffee
I just wanted to be somewhere
Anywhere
Different

I drain the last vestiges of lukewarm liquid
The waitress returns to take away my empty cup
"How was it?" she asks
"Amazing", I reply
It's the only language some people understand

As I walk back home
I reflect on how much I've enjoyed this simple pleasure
Until so recently taken for granted
Just a small part of a daily routine
But today, truly
Amazing

Turns out she was right all along

Worse Things Happen At Sea

Having followed City's Champions League journey from its outset – each year booking a cancellable hotel in the city chosen to host the final, each year duly having to cancel it – in 2021 we finally made it through to the showpiece match. During lockdown.

For most of that season, games had been played in empty stadia, but eventually a tentative, experimental return to allowing supporters to attend began. And it was decreed that 10,000 fans could attend the final, where City would face Chelsea. With two English teams competing, you might have thought that UEFA would relocate the match to Wembley, so that supporters would at least be spared the ordeal of having to take a flight, clearly the mode of transport most conducive to spreading the virus, but oh no. Couldn't possibly inconvenience the UEFA bigwigs. So Porto it was. Under normal circumstances a wonderful city to visit, but on this occasion I was pretty apprehensive. Still, I wasn't going to miss this for the world. Or was I?

I've travelled all over Europe following the Blues
The story's always the same, eventually we lose
But this year the final in Porto awaits
Though it should have been Wembley, and that really grates
But we all know UEFA don't give a toss about the fans
So I'm forced to make short-notice travelling plans

I get some right grief at home, "You must be insane!
The last thing you want is to get on a plane
After being so careful, to do this is criminal"
But I convince myself that the risk is minimal
"It's once-in-a-lifetime" keeps flashing through my brain
If I don't do this, will I ever do anything again?
All passengers have to be tested, I've been double jabbed
So I purchase my ticket before they're all grabbed
And I book myself onto the Sheikh's free flight
Travelling back in the middle of the night

But just to show how far we still are from normality
I need a PCR test, but that's just a formality
It costs 95 quid, what an absolute racket
Opportunist bastards making a packet
I just write the cash off, what else can you do
And next morning the test result e-mail comes through

Positive
Fuck!

I'm gobsmacked, stunned, it's properly shocked me
I've been so obsessively cautious, even friends have mocked me
It must be a mistake! I trawl all over the net
To find this thing's about as accurate as you can get

"How can this have happened?" I repeatedly ask
Some twat in the Arndale who wouldn't wear a mask?
The girl in the coffee shop? The restaurant waiter?
The emergency dentist? Wish I'd left it till later…
But whatever it was, my passport's back in the drawer
And I'll be watching on telly, feeling sick to the core

We're favourites to win but we don't turn up
Pep's inexplicable tinkering buggers us up
Chelsea, deservedly, walk off with the cup

I feel like we've bottled it and I'm hardly alone
But at least I don't have a long journey home
And yes it's a sickener, but though it may seem perverse
If we'd won I'd have felt a hundred times worse
Cos then the pain of not being there would never be erased
I'd have been bitter and twisted for the rest of my days

But for now I'm infected, apparently, so how do I feel?
I'm an ageing asthmatic, it's not really ideal
I'd been fearing to catch it would mean certain death
But not once was I ever even remotely out of breath
Maybe it's the vaccine, maybe it's luck
But frankly, my dear, I don't give a fuck

And as for the Blues, we'll come back from this pain
Now we've reached our first final we can do it again
And I'll be there for sure if we make it next season[1]
Maybe, sometimes, things happen for a reason

> [1] *It actually took two years for us to get to the final again, but I was present and correct in Istanbul to watch us finally lift the trophy. And complete the ultimate treble. Someone really should write a book about it...*

THAT'S JUST SILLY

Probably my favourite poems to write are the ones which are totally absurd. They're usually the product of a fevered imagination, a desire to take a concept and stretch it so it becomes as silly as possible, more like a comedy sketch than a poem. Their genesis can be absolutely anything, a throwaway line in a conversation, a news item, something I notice when wandering round the streets, an advert, a snippet of a TV programme...

So many things make me think, "That might make a poem" but relatively few of them actually do, and the original idea gets stored away, never to be resurrected. But every now and then, I get a few couplets together, the idea gets a bit of traction and away I go on a flight of fancy, to a place where no rational person would want to tread. I love it there.

My favourite audience reaction from any of the stuff I've done over the years is absolute bewilderment, that "what the fuck was that all about?" look. I've seen it a lot and I love it. Much more satisfying than laughter. And, to be fair, much more common than laughter. But laughter's ok as well. Anything but indifference...

King Dong

I've always found something absurdly comedic about the flashermac brigade, although I appreciate that it isn't necessarily that funny if you're on the receiving end. Though it probably usually is.

This is a nostalgic piece which recalls those wonderful days when you could walk around exposing yourself in public, and people would react with polite laughter or with a sheepish grin. Try it nowadays and the police will bundle you into the back of a van and kick the shit out of you. Apparently…

This poem tells the ultimately tragic story of an extremely well-endowed exhibitionist.

He rejoiced in the nickname of Supersize Sam
And was widely renowned for not giving a damn
He first whipped it out in the queue for the tram
In front of this woman pushing a pram
She said, "Fuck me! It's like a battering ram
Can I just take a picture to send to me mam?"
King Dong

He'd been loitering in Tescos for quite a while
When he spotted a woman of impeccable style
An investment manager in the Square Mile
He gave her an eyeful in the frozen food aisle
She gazed at his weapon and observed with a smile
"That's highly impressive – very much top quartile"
King Dong

When he sat down for brunch in his local café
Within seconds his clothing was in disarray
And with a flourish befitting Lord Olivier
He slapped his meat out on the breakfast tray
An old dear at the counter said, "What a splendid display…
Can I have one of those to take away?"
King Dong

It was the final question at his job interview
What d'you do in your spare time? – the perfect cue
The dong was unleashed without further ado
Then he swung it around like a cowboy's lasso
She shrieked with delight and said, "This interview's through
You start on Monday... and bring your friend too"
King Dong

At a wedding reception on the edge of a lake
The happy couple were cutting the cake
In what would prove to be a fatal mistake
He whipped out his one-eyed trouser snake
The groom caught a glimpse and said, "Oh, for fuck sake!"
And knew straight away what action to take
On King Dong

The dong was lopped off with one swish of the blade
Which left him in desperate need of first-aid
But the drunken guests didn't have a clue *what* to do
"Has anyone got any superglue?"
By the time the paramedics arrived
He'd lost too much blood to be revived
King Dong

The church filled with mourners who'd always remember
The spectacular sight of his legendary member
At the end of the service they began reminiscing
But he went into the furnace with his pride and joy missing
Now it's preserved for posterity in a jar on the shelf
A sad, shrivelled, shadow of its once-glorious self
King Dong

Pure Cremation TV

I was watching one of those dedicated 60s and 70s music channels, and every ad break seemed to feature low-cost cremation services. You can't say they don't know their market. But one of them, Pure Cremation, really stood out. It invited viewers to tune into "Pure Cremation TV." I thought to myself, how the hell can you have a TV channel which shows wall to wall cremations? What sort of sick bastards are going to watch that?

So I googled Pure Cremation TV and found that the "TV" bit was just some animated films depicting their services and illustrating how comforting it was for the relatives to have everything taken care of with no fuss. It was all very tasteful. But by then it was too late, because I'd already got into my head this concept of a TV channel which broadcast live cremations 24/7. How would they get people to watch it? This is what I came up with.

Lockdown life, afternoon TV
Where the ads are all targeted at old folk - like me
Worried about care in case you get ill?
Have you got yourself an up-to-date will?
Get cash from your home with equity release
Beef up your hearing with this invisible earpiece
Stannah stairlifts and smoke alarm sensors
Saga cruises and funeral expenses
But then I saw something brand new to me
An advert for Pure Cremation TV

Getting buried's terribly outdated
It's so much slicker to be cremated
Just look how smoothly those curtains close
And at least your body won't decompose
On our channel 24/7
You can watch the deceased *en route* to heaven
Though if they're politicians or estate agents or paparazzi
Or in any way connected to MUFC
Then they're far more likely to be
On a steeply downward trajectory

For just £5 a month, not a penny more
We'll also deliver straight to your door
Our celebrity cremation magazine *Goodbye (exclamation mark)*
This month's cover star's Joan of Arc
We ask, "Can the newly departed still hear us?"
While celebs show off the deluxe interiors
Of their crass and tacky handmade coffins
The perfect vehicles to see them off in
And you can watch their exits with sadistic glee
Dead and exclusive on Pure Cremation TV

You might think the market for our channel's small
Seen one cremation, seen 'em all
But that just shows how wrong you can be
'Cos here on Pure Cremation TV
We ramp up the glitz and glamour
The vicar wears pants like MC Hammer
Coffins in the colours of the occupant's team
Psychedelic curtains like an acid-fuelled dream
And as for that morose organ music
In our transmissions we never use it
'Cos in accordance with public demand
Those dismal dirges are totally banned
We play KC and his Sunshine Band
So you can wave goodbye to dear grandpa
With "That's the way, aha aha
I like it, aha aha"

And he'll shuffle off the mortal coil
In an atmosphere like a carnival
With strobe lights flashing and a disco ball
In these depressing days where better to be
Than knocking back beers on your settee
While watching Pure Cremation TV
As the boy Palmer said with his final breath
Might as well face it, you're Addicted To Death

Imadickhead.com

This is about people who perpetrate idiotic mindless acts of stupidity and somehow manage to get compensation for it as a result of the intervention of immoral ambulance chasing bastards.

The world that we live in moves at such a pace
You can have a little mishap any time, any place
You might think, "Shit happens" and just get on with your day
But at Imadickhead.com we don't see things that way
Cos even if you're completely to blame
Where there's a dickhead, there's always a claim

I fired up me new barbecue to cook a few bangers
And some sirloin steaks – Aberdeen Angus
I brought the barbie inside when the weather turned dire
And half an hour later me house was on fire
My insurers wouldn't cough up, said it was all my fault
Made me feel like some sort of braindead dolt
But Imadickhead.com said I've got justified cause
Cos the manual never stated, "Not to be used indoors"

I'd just put some new laces in my favourite shoes
I was running for the bus, there was no time to lose
I tripped over a loose end and came to serious grief
Me nose got smashed in and I lost half me teeth
I said, "It wasn't my fault, I did nothing wrong
It was those laces you sold me, they were way too long"
I looked at the wrapper the following morning
No sign of a health and safety warning
The conclusion to this saga's already foregone
And I'll be getting a payout from Imadickhead.com

I fancied a change from breakfast marmalade
So I bought this peanut butter in my local arcade
The label on the jar said guaranteed satisfaction
But I soon fell victim to an allergic reaction
I was rushed into hospital a few minutes later
Where I spent two weeks on a ventilator
Now I want compensation, no ifs no buts
Cos the label never said, "This product may contain nuts"

The bloke in the shop said his binoculars were simply the best
So I rushed home eager to put 'em to the test
That night I spied on my neighbour getting undressed
But the bitch dobbed me in, now I'm under arrest
She said I was a filthy disgusting perv
I said, "You've got a fucking nerve
If you don't want people watching you should close the blinds"
But the magistrate slapped me with a bloody great fine
Buying those binoculars turned me into a peeping tom
So I'll be seeking redress from Imadickhead.com

I was on me way to watch City away at Stoke
When I noticed the zip on me flies had broke
I thought I can't walk round like this, I look a right tit
So I went into Wilkos and bought a repair kit
A pack of needles with cotton in appropriate shades
With a new zip - and scissors with supersharp blades
But in me rush to mend me pants in time for kick off
The scissors slipped through the fabric and I cut me dick off
"What the hell were you thinking of?" asked the nurse
"Well, the instructions never said to take your trousers off first"
Now me wife calls me Bobbitt cos me manhood's almost gone
But I'll get some serious compo from Imadickhead.com

Embarrassed or ashamed? We don't care
If you've done something stupid we'll pin the blame elsewhere
Whether you're living on the breadline or frightfully posh
We'll always find a loophole to get you some dosh
Cos keeping dickheads in clover, that's our mission
And we only take 40% in commission
So if you're a major league fuckwit or just trying it on
You're guaranteed a payout from Imadickhead.com

Celebrity Shags

In a moment when the balance of my mind was disturbed – probably due to a surfeit of red wine, although it could have been gin – I had this idea for a poem about celebrities who had sex together purely because their surnames rhymed. I wanted to make the pairings as unlikely as possible. Unfortunately, for the first verse to make any sense, I needed Des O'Connor to die.

Obviously, I would never have wished such a thing on dear old Des, a man impossible to dislike, but his impressive longevity meant that by the time the poem was ready to go, some of the references were so out of date as to be obsolete. There must be lots more potential rhyming copulators out there but, given my aversion to all aspects of modern-day celebrity culture, then they're lost on me. So you'll just have to make do with this meagre assortment.

I've seen a video of Madonna
Having sex with Des O'Connor
For three whole hours he was off and on her
No wonder the poor old boy's a goner

Moaning minnie Alan Hansen
He thinks he's perfect, the way he rants on
Shame he couldn't keep his pants on
When propositioned by Esther Rantzen

Can you believe that Halle Berry
Bonked all four of Mungo Jerry?
She also snogged that Katy Perry
But she got the brush off from John Terry[1]

Prince, that pint-sized Casanova
Shagged Maria Sharapova
She's a bigger unit than Betty Stove[2]
How the fuck did that dwarf get his leg over?

> [1] *This was quite a satirical line back in 2011*
> [2] *1970's Dutch tennis player, unusually tall and powerful for the era*

Man Flu

It's a widely acknowledged fact that, whatever the ailment, the symptoms always manifest themselves more severely in men than in women - especially when it comes to colds. Despite our unbending determination to soldier on and suffer in silence, things can sometimes get so bad that we're forced reluctantly to spend a day or two in bed and forego the many and varied pleasures of going to work.

The lack of sympathy we get for our plight never ceases to amaze me. I hope that this poem helps to raise awareness of just how tough we have it.

I've got this brutal hacking cough
I just can't shake the bastard off
And I seem to have lost my sense of smell
Sounds like Covid, bloody hell
I'd better take a lateral flow
The result comes through, oh please God no
It's negative
Shit!
I must've got Man Flu
Get on the phone and call the nurse
And while you're at it book that hearse
Cos there's never been an illness worse
Than Man Flu

I've spent the last three days in bed
I'm feeling like the living dead
My nose is streaming, I've got the shivers
My voice is huskier than Joan Rivers
I've already used up way more tissues
Than a man with wanking addiction issues
This evil bug has wiped me out
I can barely whisper, never mind shout
My days are numbered without a doubt
It's Man Flu

I think I need a ventilator
My throat feels like I've swallowed a grater
This headache's minging, I'm in such pain
But not once will you hear me complain
Cos in adversity I'm always stoic
My fighting spirit defines heroic
My temperature must be 105
I can't believe I'm still alive
But I'll need a miracle to survive
This Man Flu

My wife keeps telling me I'll be ok
That's easy enough for her to say
She says that women have problems too
Well yes, I know, of course you do
But even when you're in the wars
With periods, childbirth, menopause
You still should thank your lucky stars
You'll never know the misery caused
By Man Flu

Whaddya mean, "If you want a cup of tea, get it your fucking self"?

I'm An Accountant

I spent many years working as an actuary. As with all professions, we were perceived as extremely boring, and this was pretty much spot-on. The most common joke about us was that we started out as accountants but found it too exciting. Not exactly a sidesplitter. There was no point writing a poem about actuaries because most people don't know what we do and we're notoriously useless at trying to describe it. So I thought accountants would be more relatable.

I've met and worked with a lot of accountants and most of them are indeed desperately dull. But I know a few who are great fun and you'd never guess what they did for a living. This poem, about stereotypes and how not everyone conforms to them, takes it to extremes on both sides.

I've worked for the same firm all my life
So did my father and so has my wife
For the last 25 years I've dwelt
In semi-detached commuter belt
My house represents the fruit of my labours
It looks just the same as all of my neighbours
The décor is perfect for the modern age
The walls are magnolia and the carpets are beige
Sunday's the day when I wash my car
The most exciting part of my weekend by far
Cos I'm an accountant

X-Factor and *The Voice* leave me cold
I like my music a little more bold
Cutting edge rock is more my thing
Like Dire Straits, Ed Sheeran, Coldplay and Sting
I file their CDs in alphabetical order
It's part of my obsessive compulsive disorder
On the first of each month I like to unwind
By going through my bank statement line by line
It takes three or four hours but makes perfect sense
I once claimed a refund of fifty-nine pence
Cos I'm an accountant

I first met my wife on an auditing course
The balance sheet session was a *tour de force*
But in the evening I drank two halves of shandy
And she morphed into ravishing eye candy
How we ended up in bed is still a mystery
But we got it together and the rest is history
I didn't time it properly but I reckoned
I lasted two minutes and thirty seconds
She seemed disappointed when I needed a rest
I didn't tell her it was my personal best
Six months later we were man and wife
Living a perfectly ordered life
The domestic budget runs like clockwork
Her favourite pastime's doing the housework
She stacks the dishwasher with clinical precision
Marrying her was the right decision
Cos she's an accountant

At work I insist that all my staff
Religiously read The Daily Telegraph
They make childish jokes, like saying I've never had sex
That kind of thing leaves me perplexed
Cos I've shown them photos so they can see
That I've got two kids who look just like me
I do have to admit they represent
A conversion rate of fifty percent
In fact the last time I got an erection
Was when I catalogued my VAT receipt collection
Cos I'm an accountant

I'm proud of my son, he's so well-mannered
While other kids his age were out getting hammered
He was immersed in books on taxation treaties
Now he's fully qualified and he'll often beat us
At our weekly game of Trivial Pursuit
His general knowledge is beyond dispute
He lives at home though he's thirty-two
Still only speaks when he's spoken to
Look him in the eye and he'll always blush
He's never had a girlfriend but there's no rush
Cos he's an accountant

My daughter's realised all my worst fears
She's been totally off the rails for years
When she hit her teens she was sniffing glue
And necking bottles of Malibu
With her capacity for classroom disruption
Matched only by her vodka consumption
She then graduated to class A drugs
Hanging out with dealers, junkies and thugs
Now she's addicted to the scent of danger
Constantly having sex with strangers
She's constructed a comprehensive spreadsheet
Showing all the men who've crumpled her bedsheets
It's a model of clarity, you can see at a glance
Everyone who's ever been inside her pants
They're listed by date and alongside their name
Is the size of their cock and how often she came
Full details of every night of passion
Are set out in concise and logical fashion
Each relevant factor is weighted and then
She gives them a final mark out of ten
Its scientifically accurate and thoroughly checked
But then what else would you expect?
Cos she's an accountant

Jurgen Klopp's Teeth

A couple of years ago I was watching the Liverpool manager being interviewed on TV and thought to myself, "I'm sure his teeth didn't used to be that white." And ever since then I've found them to be incredibly distracting, so much so that I often can't concentrate on what he's actually saying. Sometimes this can be a very good thing indeed, but in fairness I do usually enjoy listening to him, which is not the case with many of his counterparts.

This prime example of extreme dentistry has become such an obsession that I felt obliged to put together a poem in celebration of Jurgen's spectacular gnashers.

He travelled over from Dortmund to manage The 'Pool
And the boys on the Kop thought, "this guy looks pretty cool"
With his heavy metal football and baseball cap
He came across as a rather endearing chap
But for years his appearance had caused him concern
And now he could sort it, cos he'd have money to burn
He decided the treatment he most needed was dental
But the dentist he chose was right fucking mental
Whose teeth whitening methods were scarily experimental
The world is awash with incredible sights
Like Niagara Falls and the Northern Lights
The Hanging Gardens of Babylon and the Great Barrier Reef
But nothing compares with Jurgen Klopp's teeth

When he turned up at training that Monday morning
The players said, "Fuck me boss, you could have give us a warning"
They fled from the ground before any damage was done
Crying, "Jesus, it's like staring straight at the sun!"
They returned wearing shades with maximum UV protection
But still no-one dared look in Jurgen's direction
They saw their physio in tears, they asked what was upsetting her
"I only glanced at his mouth, now I've fucked up me retina!"
It's a miracle no-one else came to serious grief
When exposed to the terrors of Jurgen Klopp's teeth

It was the title decider, the stakes were immense
The reds were one up, the situation was tense
So Jurgen set up an extra line of defence
He took up a spot behind the Liverpool net
With his dentures all ready to avert any threat
The opponents' striker burst through, the ball at his feet
He looked certain to score, just the keeper to beat
He was all set to shoot and leave the Kop in despair
When Jurgen unleashed his best grin with a dazzling glare
The striker went arse over tit, the fans sighed with relief
Their dream still alive thanks to Jurgen Klopp's teeth

Hold on for the win and the title was nailed
But with just a few minutes left the floodlights all failed
The electricians were baffled, couldn't find what was wrong
And the referee got fed up with waiting so long
He said, "I'm sorry, I know it's a terrible shame
But if they're not fixed in ten minutes, I'll abandon the game"
There was no time to lose, this was the moment of truth
And one clever chap managed to think on the hoof
"Take Jurgen upstairs and get him on the roof
It's like there's ten thousand lumens in every tooth"
He was dragged up to the gantry at considerable pace
They wired open his mouth and strapped him in place
Like a track-suited alien from outer space
The pitch was instantly bathed in glorious light
The ref said, "Just keep the cunt up there, we can play all night!"
Their opponents looked on in sheer disbelief
As the reds won the title thanks to Jurgen Klopp's teeth

The local school needed help to get GCSE passes
So they wheeled Jurgen in for the kids' science classes
The teacher wanted to simulate a solar eclipse
So Jurgen smiled for a while then they stitched up his lips
But a chemical reaction caused by lack of aeration
Saw his mouth overcome by a burning sensation
It turned out that his dentist couldn't really be trusted
Cos those teeth got so hot he spontaneously combusted
He was reduced in a flash to a big pile of ashes
Topped off with his brilliant thermonuclear gnashers
All the parents reacted with real indignation
When their kids said they'd witnessed a classroom cremation
So a great manager's career ended up all too brief
And here ends the saga of Jurgen Klopp's teeth

And the moral of this story is DON'T FUCK WITH NATURE!

Me House Is On Fire

Not sure what brought this one about. Certainly one of the triggers was the frustration of spending an age listening to an automated answering service when I was desperate to speak to a real person. As was a self-obsessed pair of next-door neighbours from a few years back. And it all sort of mushroomed from there...

I'm on the motorway, driving back home
Me boring neighbour's droning on on the phone
He says, "My daughter's career's going really well
She's got a new job in personnel
I've just booked our holiday hotel
It was a personal favourite of Sid Waddell
My ingrowing toenail's giving me hell
And by the way, your house is on fire"
"Me house is on fire?" "Yes, your house is on fire"
"Don't talk bollocks, you bloody liar
You tell worse fibs than Aldridge Prior[1]
As a wind-up merchant you're bloody dire"
"Look, I'm telling you pal, your house is on fire"

I arrive at me road, there's smoke in the air
I'm overcome by a sense of despair
I turn into my drive and my neighbour's there
"See, I told you, your house is on fire!"
Did I forget to turn off the deep fat fryer?
Did a mouse chew through electrical wire?
Has the neighbourhood arsonist gone haywire?
Me insurance premiums'll be three times higher
I'm well and truly in the mire
I can't believe it, me house is on fire

I said, "You've dialled 999 haven't you?"
He said "I did try once but I couldn't get through,
So then I thought I'd just leave it all to you"
What else was there for me to do?

"Thank you for calling the emergency services
Please note that this call may be recorded for training and monitoring purposes
Please listen carefully to the following options before making your selection
For police, press 1
For fire brigade, press 2
For ambulance, press 3
For police and fire brigade, press 4
For police and ambulance, press 5
For fire brigade and ambulance, press 6
For police, fire brigade and ambulance, press 7
To hear the options again, press 8
Or, if you wish to speak to an operative, please continue to hold"

Eventually a voice emerges in the distance
Asking me how he can be of assistance
I said, "Me house is on fire!"
"Your house is on fire?"
"Yes, me house is on fire!"
"Well, can you tell me what service you require?"
My reserves of patience were about to expire
I said, "What the fuck do you think, me house is on fire!"

"Sounds like you need the fire brigade to me
But I'm afraid we haven't got anyone free
Apart from our work experience trainee
They're all out at an emergency
A pedigree cat's got stuck up a tree
They should be with you by half past three
Staff cutbacks have hit us hard, you see
It's all down to Brexit if you ask me
What else can I say but *c'est la vie?*"

"Are you lot taking the fucking piss?
What kind of emergency service is this?
My life's possessions are going up in smoke
And you seem to think it's some kind of joke
You're living in a parallel universe
I thought Northern Rail were bad but you lot are worse"

"Please try to stay calm sir, and whatever you do
Just wait for our expert fire-fighting crew
Of course you'll have items you'd like to rescue
But trying to save 'em's the worst thing you can do
We'd hate anything to happen to you
Just nip down the pub for a beer or two"

I thought, "Fuck that, me house is on fire!"
I couldn't hang around for a second more
I took a deep breath and opened the door
Belching black smoke filled the corridor
The flames came at me with a great orange roar
I heard a big bang and I hit the floor
My life flashed before me – it was all over for sure

I opened my eyes and let out a scream
Bloody hell, what a terrible dream
Look at me, I'm dripping in sweat
The sheets and pillows are soaking wet
I must say this bedroom's unusually warm
Hang on, is that the smoke alarm?
Fuckin hell…

> 1. *A character in Viz comic, "Aldridge Prior the Hopeless Liar" routinely fabricates ludicrous stories with his every utterance. Very much in the same envelope as Kenny Dalglish Snr in Phoenix Nights.*

Televisual Feast

The death of Queen Elizabeth in 2022 came against a backdrop of a family in disarray. It does make you wonder whether she simply lost the will to live, worn down by the tasteless antics of her fellow Royals. Maybe seeing Prince Charles' charity beset by "cash for honours" allegations was the final straw, coming so soon after the nauseating self-pitying twattishness of the gruesome twosome and the unspeakable behaviour of Prince Andrew.

If only she'd been able to persuade her motley crew to do what dysfunctional families always used to do – appear on the Jeremy Kyle Show. It might not have helped, but it would have made great telly. My imagination ran away with me on this one, depicting the Queen as a foul-mouthed chavvy Cockney and Prince Charles as a wife-beating yobbo. We can but dream...

Two years have gone by since Jeremy Kyle
Last darkened our screens with his programme so vile
He was pulling legs off spiders in his palatial home
When his agent excitedly got on the phone
You would not believe the public demand
To see Big Betty Windsor and the rest of the gang
So I've been on the blower to ITV
Who've offered to cough up an astronomical fee
If you'll come out of retirement for just one show
And for that kind of money, how could Jezza say no?

The trailers ran for night after night
And whipped up in the public a huge appetite
Is Meghan a bully, is Charlie Boy racist
Who is Harry's dad, is Andrew really a rapist?
They finally assembled in Studio Five
Each hoping to bury the others alive
Meghan's chance came first, and how well she took it
Enough crocodile tears to fill an ice-bucket
It was just like they'd taught her in drama school
But not everyone was so easily fooled

The Queen said, "Fuck me, this is worse than X-Factor
She's feigning sincerity like a crap D-list actor"
Meghan recoiled in horror, "Whaddya you mean, D-list?"
To which Betty replied, "Well, there isn't an E-list
And just listen here, you jumped-up prima donna
Much more of this, and you'll soon be a goner
Cos the firm's on the warpath, don't say I didn't warn you
And you'd better piss off back to California
Cos if you keep behaving in this diabolical manner
We'll hire a French taxi driver - like we did for Diana"

Jezza said, "Calm down, Your Majesty, or can I call you Bet
Can you remember the moment when you two first met?"
"Yeah, she breezed into my gaff with the distinctive odour
Of a narcissistic shallow freeloader
She said, "Why don't you like me?" I said, "I'll be brutally frank
You're a vacuous, self-obsessed gold-digging Yank"
Harry sprang to her defence like an obedient pup
"There's no need for that gran, just shut the fuck up"
Betty cried, "Hear that, Charles? Your boy's right out of line"
But Charlie said, "Why should I care, he's not one of mine
Don't you remember, his real dad's been paid off
And vanished forever, cos that was the trade-off
We gave you a chance boy, and you bloody well blew it
You'll spend the rest of your days as plain Harry Hewitt"

Harry leapt from his seat, incensed and outraged
As security stepped up to the side of the stage
Jezza said, "Stay where you are boys, this is pure TV gold"
But then Charlie Boy's headbutt laid Harry out cold
Charlie said, "Who else wants some, me right hook's a killer
I practise it every night on Camilla"
Andrew played to the crowd, "Told you Charlie was scum
He's a two-timing tree-hugger as out of touch as they come
With an indecent proposal to get rich folk excited
Give his charity a wedge and next year you'll be knighted"

"Put your own house in order!" was Charlie's response
"Don't try to deny it, we all know you're a nonce
Now you're out on your ear but no need to feel bitter
You can start over again as the new Gary Glitter"
Andrew smiled and expressed not a single regret
"I'll come out of this smelling of roses...no sweat
You losers do what you like, I'll always eclipse it
With my new TV series called *Andrew'll Fix It*
There'll be after-show parties at a secret address
Though I won't be there myself, I'll be in Pizza Express"

As a TV spectacular the show had no equal
And the bosses insisted, "We must do a sequel!"
But Jezza said, "No way, I just couldn't risk it
We've had some right tossers on here...but this lot take the biscuit"

The Bride Of Dracula

Those bloody Americans again. I was brought up on "Penny for the Guy" where you at least had to expend a modest amount of creative energy to get the neighbours to cough up a few coppers. But when "Trick or Treat" took a hold, the equation became "give us some money or we'll throw raw eggs at your windows". You can't deny that this is an outstanding business model but it does feel as though it might be steering youngsters towards a life of crime and extortion.

I'm pretty sure that the terrible punchline has been nicked subconsciously from a decades old copy of The Beano. There can be no finer provenance.

It's Trick Or Treat night, those kids are the scourge of this town
But I need something to give 'em, or else they'll burn me house down
Better take a quick trip to the shops, I suppose
And I bought in a few bags of Haribos
The young 'uns turned out in costumes, all embracing the occult
But I couldn't take my eyes off the accompanying adult
A princess of darkness, albeit without a tiara
Though I thought that she'd - possibly - overdone the mascara
I said, "Your Halloween costume's truly spectacular"
But that was no fancy dress…she was the Bride Of Dracula

I went back inside, thought about her no more
But half an hour later came a knock at the door
This vision of beauty was there on her own
Saying, "I was hoping I might just catch you alone
It was so nice that you bought the kids all those sweets
They didn't half do the trick, so now it's time for *your* treat"
There's a saying I learnt whilst living down South
"Never look a gift vampire in the mouth"
She looked bloody fit, to use the vernacular
So into my house came the Bride Of Dracula

She was alluring…enticing…it was hard not to leer
I said, "Can I get you a drink, how about a cold beer?"
"Ooh that's very kind, aren't you quite the charmer
But if you don't mind, I'd prefer something warmer"
I said, "How hot do you want it? I'll make sure it's just right"
"Ooh, about 98.6 fahrenheit"
Her milky white skin had a sheen of translucence
But would that tightly-laced bodice prove a bit of a nuisance?
Still, I do love a challenge and I was ready to tackle her
So upstairs I went with the Bride Of Dracula

She pinned me to the bed, I thought, "Ooh she's dominant"
Then I noticed her front teeth were unusually prominent
What I'd thought were false fangs were now all too realistic
The look in her eyes was deranged and sadistic
I'd thought she had such a delightful persona
But she intended to make me an involuntary blood donor
I've not been so scared since I first saw the Daleks
I fled to the kitchen…but I'd run out of garlic
And hurtling behind me was this sinister cackler
I was quaking with terror at the Bride Of Dracula

She said, "What's all the panic, don't be such a wuss
Just a quick love bite and you'll be one of us
And please stop all that screaming, it's like Beatlemania"
I said, "Will you just fuck off back to Transylvania!"
But she was a woman possessed, no words could appease her
So I grabbed a T-bone steak from the back of the freezer
I flung it hard at her head, there was no point in waiting
But she ducked…and it went straight through my favourite oil painting
She slumped stricken to the floor, my relief off the chart
I'd finished her off with a steak…through the art…

ACKNOWLEDGEMENTS

Manchester – indeed, Greater Manchester - has long been justly renowned for its fabulous creative scene. But bubbling beneath the iconic venues with their household names and headline makers are an absolute wealth of events which provide performance opportunities for allcomers, whatever their genre or experience.

It's a world I'd never have discovered if I hadn't belatedly decided to have a go myself, and it's been a revelation. And while I love getting up on stage, there's often as much if not more pleasure to be had in watching other people do their thing, whether it's spoken word, comedy, music or whatever. It's a constant source of wonderment to me that there are so many people out there where you've no idea what their daily lives are like, but put 'em behind a microphone and they're bloody brilliant.

So a big thanks to the band of people who make the effort to provide a platform for all manner of creative types, and in particular to the following, who've been a real help to me personally, always supportive and sometimes even enthusiastic. (Some of these events are no longer running but are still remembered with affection.) Here's to Ilaria, Lisa and Alicia (and Adam, Amy and Zoe before them) at Verbose; Ilaria (again) at Just Stories; Becca and Jas at Blue Balloon Theatre; Andy N, Amanda and Steve at Speak Easy; Rob at Punk In Drublic; Paul, Mel and Tony at Word Central; Will and Michaela at Switchblade Society; Caroline at Heard Storytelling; Simone at Long Story Short; Jay at Nook Open Door; John at the Old Pint Pot; Jase at Comedy Balloon; Alex at Retro Bar; Tuesday Tony at Thirsty Scholar; Culain at Rhyming Words, Glossop; Ian at Write Oud Loud, Wigan; Romina and Stuart at Natter, Bolton; Damien at The Station, Ashton and, further afield, Tara at Off The Tap, Maidenhead and Debz at Testify in Zoomland.

Finally, respect and love to Lindsey for being brave enough to come along and support from time to time. It's always amusing (though sometimes distracting) to see her scanning round the audience trying to see who I've mortally offended this time. She always seems to find someone. To be honest, I'd be disappointed if she didn't...

OTHER STUFF

You can find videos of many of the poems in this book on my YouTube channel "Garden Shed Poetry By Steve Mingle". The videos are somewhat primitive (although the shed's quite nice) but I'm topping them up with a few live performances filmed by people who know what they're doing. If I get a few more subscribers then I'll try to keep it a bit more up to date.

I really can't be doing with social media but during lockdown I was reluctantly persuaded to participate in Instagram in order to keep up with what was going on in zoom spoken word world. You can find me masquerading as vlad.the.inhaler57 where I post very occasionally and only when I think I've got something interesting to share. If only others would do the same thing...

Finally, if you're into football (especially Manchester City) then you might enjoy some of my other publications...

Lows, Highs and Balti Pies – Manchester City Ruined My Diet (2004)

Allison Wonderland – Mastermind Of Maine Road's Golden Age (2008)

From Balti Pies To The Biggest Prize – The Transformation Of Manchester City (2013)

A Football Fling (2015)

When England Ruled The World – Four Years that Shaped The Modern Game (2016)

50 Years Of Manchester City – The Best And Worst Of Everything (2017)

Chasing Immortality – Manchester City's Ultimate Season (2023)

They're all available on Amazon, and other online retailers, as well as in the odd physical store here and there. You can get them direct from the publishers (The History Press for the first three, Pitch Publishing for the rest) or just get in touch with me directly to get discounted signed copies. I've got loads of the buggers cluttering up the office...